You Can Change

YOU CAN CHANGE

Stories from Angola Prison and the Psychology of Personal Transformation

Mark W. Baker

FORTRESS PRESS

MINNEAPOLIS

YOU CAN CHANGE
Stories from Angola Prison and the Psychology of Personal Transformation

Cover image: © Shutterstock 2019 / bird flying by Jacob_09
Cover design: Laura Drew, Drew Design

Print ISBN: 978-1-5064-5564-8
eBook ISBN: 978-1-5064-5565-5

In memory of Dwight Case

Contents

Acknowledgments

I am grateful to Burl Cain and the inmates of the Louisiana State Penitentiary for inviting me into their lives and trusting me with their stories. A special thank you goes to Assistant Warden Cathy Fontenot, who gave Warden Cain a copy of my previous book, and to Mrs. Jonalyn Cain, who actually read it and convinced her husband to let me come for a visit. I am grateful for the valuable input of Dr. Michael Hallett and Dennis Shere, and for Dr. Byron Johnson's important work that pointed the way. Thank you to Dr. Scott Weimer, Dr. Mack Harden, Jim Hart of Hartline Literary Agency, Mike Broyles of AWANA, and Dr. Rick Stedman for their suggestions and help in getting this book into the hands of readers. I am grateful for the support and insights of Dr. Don Morgan, J. D. Hinton, Dwight Case, Dennis Palumbo, Doug Richardson, and all my friends and colleagues at the La Vie Counseling Centers in Pasadena, California. As the inmates at Angola say, "This is a community," and I am grateful for mine inspiring me to do good in the world.

Introduction

People can change, but sometimes it's not easy. Surely you've heard people say "I can't help it—that's just the way I am" or "Why even bring it up to Mom? You know she won't change." And hasn't every well-meaning mother of a bride-to-be warned her with the age-old maxim, "Never marry a man expecting him to change"?

As the director of a large counseling center, I have listened to hundreds of emotionally open and deeply spiritual people confess to me that despite the genuineness of their desire to change, they continue to struggle with behavior that is both dysfunctional and unspiritual. In the past, if you asked me "Can people really change?" I would have responded, "Well, I like to say that people can grow." For over twenty-five years as a psychologist, I have witnessed all of my clients—and most of them have been genuinely spiritual people—work very hard to become better people. But because significant change requires significant discipline and effort, I have preferred to use the word *growth* rather than *change* to describe that process.

But that was before I went to the Louisiana State Penitentiary in Angola, Louisiana. In that surprising place, I saw with my own eyes that people can absolutely change, and change for good. The stories of personal transformation and change I am about to tell you are all true. But brace yourself, because we are about to take a journey into some dark and difficult places. You are going to hear about the lives of people who were so broken and dysfunctional that no one thought they could ever change. But they did. And their stories are so compelling that they changed me, too. But first, let me tell you how I ended up in a place like the maximum-security prison in Angola.

When I started to reflect on whether or not people could change, I realized I might learn more from the people who needed change the most. This led me to look into the lives of people with some of the most difficult challenges you can imagine: those who grew up in poverty, with little education, surrounded by violence, and then ended up in prison. What I discovered is that people in the worst circumstances imaginable can change. Spiritual and psychological principles of change help explain their personal transformations, and you can benefit from those principles as well. In this book, we will walk alongside the people society gave up on because they were considered too bad and too far gone to ever change. But they did. If the inmates serving life sentences at the largest maximum-security prison in America can change, anyone can.

Throughout the book I will be using examples of personal transformation taken from the lives of the inmates at the men's prison in Angola, Louisiana. But most of the principles of change you will read about here apply to both men and women equally. And even though all of the stories you will read about are completely true, most of them are pretty dramatic. Thankfully, we can all learn something from the lives of these people without having to go through what they did ourselves. They would want it that way, and I'm sure you will too.

1

Can a Person Really Change?

Ashanti Witherspoon had an unusual job. What *wasn't* unusual was the CPR training he provided to community centers or his motivational lectures on the evils of drugs and violence he regularly presented to inner-city youth—a number of community organizers do that. What *was* unusual about Ashanti's job was that after the end of his workday he would load his gear into his van and drive back to Angola, Louisiana, where he would pass through the gates of the Louisiana State Penitentiary and admit himself back into his cell, where he was serving a seventy-five-year sentence for armed robbery. Ashanti completed his job every day, and returned to prison every day, without a single guard accompanying him.

By the time he served twenty-five years in the maximum-security prison at Angola, Ashanti had advanced to such a position of responsibility that part of his job description was to go out into the community and try to be a positive influence on young men and women who still had a chance at a life of freedom. He said it was to "try to give something back." This arrangement was so unusual that he was the subject of a documentary film. I can still remember how the camera captured him, standing in the parking lot of Bank One in downtown Baton Rouge, after one of his presentations. As he stood there with no chains, no orange jumpsuit, and no armed guards around him, the documentary producer asked him the most logical question anyone could ask at that moment.

"Why don't you try to get away?"

Ashanti calmly replied, "There wouldn't be any problem for me to walk away. But the point is I've changed. The thing that I need to do is to be free. Escaping won't give me any type of freedom. Escaping, I'm still on the run, and I'm still trapped, I'm still bound by the same things that I was bound by twenty-five years ago. I want real freedom. I want to be able to walk out of prison and actually say that I'm free."

Within three years of making that statement, that is exactly what happened. George Ashanti Witherspoon was paroled and is now a free man—a very rare occurrence for those incarcerated at the Louisiana State Penitentiary. He was so obviously a changed person that the parole board had no problem releasing him back into society where he could continue doing good. And that is precisely what he is doing today. As his website, societyofservantleaders.com, notes, "Since his return to society he has owned several businesses, been an associate pastor for nine years, hosted his own talk show . . . and travels as an international speaker. He received his doctorate in Theology in January, 2013." Ashanti's story of personal change is amazing, especially for a man who lived almost twenty-eight years in a maximum-security prison.

Prisons: Where We Send People We Have Given Up On

The United States incarcerates people at a higher rate than any other country in the world—by far. We have more than two million people locked up, and we release about two thousand back into society every single day. Within three years, 66 percent of those will be reincarcerated. Sadly, it doesn't look like very many of them are changed.

In most cases, prisons are horrible places. Generally, they are simply holding cells for people we don't believe can change. To protect themselves from each other (and in some cases the guards), the prisoners form racial gangs, which offer some sort of control over the brutality and chaos. It's really pretty simple. In order to survive, a prisoner must know immediately who has *got his back* when he arrives in prison. And the quickest way to sort out friend versus foe is to identify with your race. Black prisoners join black gangs, the Hispanic prisoners join Hispanic gangs, and white prisoners rush to the Aryan gangs—all in an effort simply to stay alive. Many people think that prisons are filled with gang members from street gangs, but actually most gangs outside of prisons were formed on the inside of prisons as a matter of survival. Then the gang culture was transmitted to the outside once they were released. After years of research on America's prisons, journalist Alan Elsner concluded, "Without question, prisons are the most racially segregated as well as the most racist places in America."[1]

From my perspective as a psychologist, I determined that rehabilitation in America's prisons is not failing—it is rarely even being attempted. When a person has committed a serious crime, we appear to have decided that change is not possible, so we lock that person away. Our Departments of Corrections aren't trying to correct anything; they are simply punishing people for acting badly. It is possible to make a moral justification for that, but it isn't even in the ballpark of trying to help people change.

Then I came across a documentary film, *The Farm*, which was nominated for an Academy Award. Director Jonathan Stack followed the lives of several inmates at the Louisiana State Penitentiary and told their moving stories of personal transformation from lives of crime and murder to lives of service and compassion. These people, who had once been selfish criminals, were now dedicated to helping others with such optimism and hope that it was hard to comprehend it. This type of personal transformation was so incredible to me that I had to go and see it for myself. After a few months of a persuasive email campaign on my part, one of the assistant wardens, Cathy Fontenot, finally agreed to allow me to visit Angola. I could hardly believe what I found once I got there.

Angola

The Louisiana State Penitentiary is the largest maximum-security prison in the United States. It currently holds more than 6,200 inmates, 95 percent of whom will never leave. The vast majority of the prisoners are serving life sentences, and they will die in Angola, because they have committed murder, rape, or armed robbery. These men have done very bad things and have been condemned to die in prison because society does not believe they are capable of change.

Angola not only is the country's largest maximum-security prison but was once the most brutal. Its eighteen thousand acres were formerly the site of a plantation maintained by a slave workforce; and the prison itself has such a long history of violence and a reputation for being so cruel that it was referred to as the site of modern-day slavery. The brutality was so notorious that criminals would weep when sentenced to Angola. It was well known throughout the South that no matter how tough you were, you did not want to end up here.

But then, in 1995, Burl Cain became the warden. He didn't want the job. He remained for several years in his residence at the Dixon Correctional Institute, where he was serving as warden, hoping the Angola appointment would only be temporary. Cain was aware that none of his predecessors had lasted more than a few years in their attempts to reform Angola. But despite his reservations, he accepted the challenge because he had a different vision for how this could be done—and, most importantly, a belief that people could change. Unlike many in society who believed people who commit the crimes that send them to Angola should be locked away and forgotten, Cain believed everyone should be given the opportunity for rehabilitation. As a deeply spiritual person, he was convinced that, if we give people the proper setting and apply the proper principles, corrections could be done correctly. Angola did not have to be a place of punishment and retribution; it could be a place where people could correct their ways and be transformed. This was an extremely ambitious project, but Cain was convinced he had been called to the task.

When I first arrived at Angola in 2014, rather than

finding the notoriously brutal penitentiary I had heard so much about, I was surprised to find one of the safest prisons in the country. The main prison yard is no longer a place of violence and fear but instead has become a community of opportunity and change. Guards perform their duties without guns, female visitors and staff walk freely around the prison without getting so much as a catcall, and the atmosphere within the prison is actually peaceful. Inmates work to improve themselves, help each other, and try to advance their station in life. Even though most of them will never leave Angola, they still endeavor to make better lives for themselves. As incredible as this might sound, it's all true. I know—because I was there.

Inside Angola

On my first visit inside the walls of Angola, I toured the prison with Warden Cain and his assistant, unaccompanied by any guards. Not even one. We walked freely from building to building, stopped and talked to inmates frequently, and never experienced a hint of anger or threat of violence of any kind. Quite the opposite, I watched as inmate after inmate came up to Cain and slipped him a handwritten note with a request of some kind. I admit I felt rather uncomfortable, because we were often surrounded by dozens of prisoners just milling around on the prison grounds. But it was Cain's open-door policy to allow any inmate access to him. Throughout the prison I observed signs posted instructing staff to be "ASKable," a term he coined to create an atmosphere of respect. If a prisoner had a question of any kind, it was the responsibility of every guard or staff member to stop and answer it, or to find someone who could. Anyone observing one of these signs would have one of the first principles of change I witnessed at Angola clearly recognizable right in front of them: treat people with respect, and they will want to be respectable.

As I stood there looking at this sign, I couldn't help thinking that for the most part we all have it backwards. We think that if we punish ourselves, we will change. If I restrict my food intake, I will lose weight. It doesn't work. If I force myself to stop my bad habits on New Year's Day, I can change them. It doesn't work. If we punish criminals for their misdeeds, they will give up a life of crime. That *really* doesn't work. All this seems to do is to make people feel bad about themselves, and then what do they do? More bad stuff. What I *have* seen that does work is that treating people with respect changes them.

The opposite of punishing people is not rewarding them—it is treating them with respect. People don't act badly because they need to be taught a lesson. Most of us already know how to act properly; we just can't seem to get out of our own way to do it. One of the biggest obstacles to personal change for all people is a lack of self-respect. Without it, we get defensive and resist change. But if others take the time to communicate that they care about what we think or feel, then we begin to feel worthy of respect as people. One of the most powerful ways to develop self-respect is to have the people around us treat us as though we deserve it. Trying to get people to change through punishment and disrespect is just backwards.

Why We Think Punishing People Helps Them to Change

Human performance varies. Sometimes we are very effective and sometimes we are not, but over time, we tend toward an average level of performance.[2] If you observe people for long enough, you will notice that all behavior tends to return to that average. You might perform very well the first time you attempt a task and not so well the second time. On the other hand, if you happen to perform poorly on one occasion, it is just as probable that the very next time you attempt the task you will do somewhat better. So when we happen to be extremely good, or extremely bad, our behavior is very likely to fall closer to average next time. That's just how life is.

If you punish someone when they are exceptionally bad, that person will very likely not be as bad the very next time they attempt that behavior—not just because you punished them but also because their behavior will naturally return toward average. And if you reward someone for being exceptionally good, while they may be motivated to repeat that behavior, unfortunately their behavior is not likely to be as good the very next time they try, for the very same reason. This is why most parents repeatedly punish their children when they are being really bad and many bosses yell at their employees when they underperform. We punish people for being bad and they aren't as bad the next time, and when we say nice things to them when they are really good their behavior slips back toward average anyway. So, tragically, because of this tendency for human behavior to return to the average, we are often reinforced for punishing others rather than praising them.

Because most of us were reared this way (and we have all

had mean bosses or teachers), we have an ingrained belief that punishing bad behavior makes people do better and helps them change. It doesn't—at least not in any lasting way. But treating them with respect does. This is what Warden Cain believes, and this is what I witnessed at Angola.

Punishing people is an attempt to control their behavior. Of course we all know it can work, but it is only effective as long as there is a constant external threat of punishment to ensure compliance. Treating people with respect inspires them to *want* to change their behavior. This can help them get at the roots of their problems and actually change from the inside out. Rather than *making* them do what you want, you inspire them to *want* what you want. No external threat of punishment is necessary, so when it works it becomes self-perpetuating and far more effective at changing a person's character than any form of external control.

Gangs for God

At one point during my first visit to Angola, I received a text from my wife. She was not thrilled with my plan to spend the weekend inside a maximum-security prison, but after agonizing over my safety with her sisters, she wanted to let me know how brave they all thought I was for being there. Just as I received her text, I was walking into the Catholic chapel in the middle of the prison. It was built and operated by inmates and, as I was becoming accustomed to, there wasn't a guard in sight. What I didn't expect to see, however, were about sixty middle school girls filing into the chapel for their confirmation class. This seemed surreal. The Catholic churches of Louisiana send over seventy confirmation classes annually to Angola as a regular part of their process of confirmation into the church. The kids were typical, giggling, unassuming teenagers eagerly awaiting spiritual instruction from what was most certainly an inmate serving a life sentence who had just stood up to speak. In that moment I couldn't help thinking that, despite what my wife and her sisters might think, I was about as brave as a middle school girl showing up for confirmation.

The next day, the warden and I attended a church service in one of the prison's eight chapels. Each chapel is run by a prison church, with a prison pastor, ministering to a prison population. As we sat there, with no guard in sight (are you getting the picture?), I thought that if these 150 inmates decided to take us hostage, there would be nothing we could do about it. They had all done bad things to other people to wind up here—what if one of them decided to do bad things to us, just because he could? Later, I shared this slightly paranoid thought with the warden's assistant. He laughed and calmly said, "Well, if one of those guys had attempted to do you harm, 149 other guys would have stopped him."

The prisoners didn't need guards threatening them with clubs, tear gas, or guns. They were holding each other accountable. Again, this felt surreal.

As I sat there in this chapel, right in the middle of a maximum-security prison (I find myself having to repeat this incredible fact), I looked around. Behind me to my right was a well-dressed woman obviously sitting with her husband attending her Sunday-morning church service just like any other Christian wife would want to do. And over to my left was a neatly dressed black inmate (there are no orange jumpsuits in Angola—the warden doesn't believe in them) wheeling in an elderly white inmate who was obviously too infirm to get to the service on his own. I observed him carefully lift his friend out of his wheelchair and gently place him into the second pew. This stereotype-shattering image of compassion went against everything I had heard about typical race-based prison behavior. He seemed genuinely concerned about the man in his care, in a way that made it clear that both of these people very much wanted to be in church that morning. As I looked around, I could see that they all did.

A prison minister named Jarail gave the sermon that morning on the passage in the Bible about Barabbas, the prisoner on death row with whom Jesus was imprisoned just before his crucifixion. Following the Passover custom at the time, Pilate, the governor of Judea, was to pardon someone on death row based upon the popular vote of the people. Surprisingly, the people clamored for Barabbas over Jesus. Pilate was uncomfortable with this choice, given the disparity in the severity of the crimes committed between the two, but when the crowd said "Let his blood be upon us and our children," he agreed. Jarail, himself imprisoned for decades, was spellbinding. His point was that God can come alongside of anyone, anywhere, and pardon that person of their sins. No one is beyond the reach of God's transforming forgiveness, and God is willing to take away any person's eternal punishment if we allow it. No pastor from the outside world, no world-renowned speaker, no one other than a prisoner such as Jarail could have delivered that sermon with as much credibility. God used a death row inmate to fulfill his purposes then, and he is still doing that today—at the largest maximum-security prison in America. I can't remember having heard a better sermon anywhere.

At one point Jarail confessed that he had committed every single crime on his rap sheet, and that he too deserved punishment. But because he had confessed his guilt and received forgiveness from God, he was now willing to spend the rest of his life trying to do only good toward everyone he knew, wherever he was, even if it was right there in Angola. When, at the end of the sermon, Jarail invited his listeners to join him in a life of doing good, almost everyone in the room went forward. These people wanted transformation. Despite their circumstances, every one of these convicted criminals wanted to change and become better people.

As the warden and I left the service, I commented how powerful an experience it had been listening to Jarail. Cain calmly said, "So, you see how it is in here? Out there, they all had gangs. And in here they have them, too. But for men like Jarail, they have gangs for God. Everybody needs an identity. If you help them, they can find identities in doing good." *Brilliant*, I thought. *Simply brilliant.* Jarail and his gang were on a mission. It was a mission to enlist as many people as they could to do good, and they were doing good like their lives depended upon it. They discouraged violence, forgave offenses, and held each other accountable for their behavior. That same day, another prisoner told me they used to call an inmate who reported someone else's bad behavior a "rat," and that inmate would very likely be killed for it. Today, inmates think of each other as good citizens for reporting bad behavior to the authorities, just like people in the outside world who care about their neighborhoods do. Angola doesn't need guards forcing people to stop doing bad things to each other; it has gangs for God helping them to do good. And they are.

My experience listening to Pastor Jarail that morning moved me to tears. The genuineness of his sermon and the passion with which he and his people came together was gripping. These people wanted transformation, and Jarail was telling them exactly how they could achieve it. The lesson for me that morning was crystal clear. It was as if a floodlight was turned on the most powerful principle for personal change that I observed at Angola: *God changes people.*

A Powerful Source for Personal Change

About 90 percent of people in America believe in God, but in recent years there has been a significant decline in attendance within every major denomination in America and a significant increase in the number of people who identify themselves as being atheist, agnostic, or "nothing in particular" when it comes to religious affiliation.[3] Most people still derive comfort from their belief in God, but there is a growing sense that many people, especially young people, don't see a personal relationship with God or religion as relevant to their daily lives. They believe that being spiritual (the belief in transcendence) is nice, but they don't believe that religion (the social institution) has any real practical significance for personal growth and change. This couldn't be further from the truth.

Dr. Lisa Miller, a clinical psychologist at Columbia University Teachers College, has been studying delinquency and psychological problems among America's youth for years, and she has come to the conclusion that spirituality is the most powerful antidote to their mental health problems available to us today.[4] Her extensive research concludes that a personal relationship with a transcendent and loving God significantly reduces the risk of depression, substance abuse, aggression, and high-risk behaviors in adolescents. Beyond that, youth that have this type of personal relationship with God get sick less often, are happier, feel more connected and less isolated, have greater resilience, and live longer.

According to Miller, the widespread use of alcohol and drugs in adolescence is a direct result of the spiritual hunger that begins to develop at that age. With the onset of adolescence comes the inclination to seek a sense of calm, the desire for a feeling of bonding with others our own age, and a love for the world or something bigger than ourselves. But in the absence of a personal relationship with a loving God, many turn to the counterfeit experiences provided by drugs and alcohol. The teens that do find a meaningful relationship with God are almost 80 percent less likely to engage in heavy substance use. They simply don't need it, because genuine spiritually actually changes people.

Miller writes from a purely scientific perspective, and she does not give any indication that she has any particular religious affiliation herself, but her research is extensive and convincing. It is clear that experiencing a personal relationship with a loving God changes you. And what is even more compelling is that adolescence and young adulthood, the primary focus of her research, is the very time of life at which most of the inmates of Angola committed the crimes that landed them there. If only they had taken their relationship with God more seriously before they ended up there, according to Miller, their lives would be totally different today. Miller is critical of religious people who view God as judgmental, and she refrains from commenting on whether any religion is better than another. What is of primary importance, she says, is a personal relationship with a loving and transcendent God. A belief in a personal and loving God is not just mystical sentimentalism; it is a powerful source for real personal change. This statement is not just coming from religious people that some might think have a biased perspective, but from the best social scientists who honestly report their research findings.

Empowered by their own prison ministers such as Jarail, the inmates at Angola have completely changed the atmosphere in the main part of the prison. Angola has a prisoner-run hospice program, prisoner-run radio station, prisoner-run magazine, prisoner-run educational program, and a world famous prisoner rodeo. If prisoners join the community of change, they can advance up the ladder of opportunity to live better lives and have meaningful employment and respect. If they don't—and some don't—then they forfeit these opportunities and fall back into the more restrictive areas of the prison, with fewer privileges and opportunities. There are always those inmates Cain refers to as predators, who consistently refuse to change. Cain believes all people can change, but he is not naïve; he also knows that some don't. Angola is not some fantasy place where very bad people are converted into very good ones through a mysterious magic. It is a community of change based upon authentic spirituality and upon giving people the respect to achieve rewards when they do well and consequences when they don't.

Group Therapy—in Prison

In order for me to understand what was really going on at Angola, Warden Cain wanted me to hear from some of the prisoners, and he insisted they be able to speak with me without him or any other staff members around.

"I want you to hear the truth," Cain said, "and you're only

going to believe it if you hear it from the inmates themselves without me listening in on the conversation."

"Okay," I agreed reluctantly, thinking to myself that this probably was a good idea psychologically, but I just wasn't sure if it was a very smart one. Despite what I had seen so far, I didn't yet feel safe enough to be left alone in a room filled with criminals serving life sentences for murder and rape. And let me tell you that just because some of them were only rapists did not make me feel any better. I could only hope that Cain knew what he was doing.

So the warden set up a meeting between me and seven inmates who were in positions of responsibility at Angola. We all filed into a small conference room, where Cain introduced me and then quickly made his exit. The first prisoner introduced himself as an alcoholic who had been at Angola for eighteen years for rape. The next two had been involved in murders surrounding drug trafficking. The inmate next to them was serving a life sentence for what he called a "crime of passion." The next guy had been at Angola for thirty-six years on a rape conviction, and next to him was an inmate seeking an appeal on his drug-trafficking and fraud convictions.

As each inmate around the table shared his story, I couldn't help feeling vulnerable. Every one of these prisoners had been involved in very serious crimes. They had faced life-and-death situations and responded violently in the past. And even though I never doubted their sincerity, I couldn't help thinking I had no idea where Warden Cain and his never-present guards were, or wondering whether anyone could hear me if I cried for help. Here I was, deep in the bowels of a maximum-security prison, alone in a room with seven inmates, most of whom were serving life sentences, and we were all acting like this was a perfectly normal and rational thing for me to be doing. It is a frightening thing to feel vulnerable and unsafe. But the longer I sat there, the more that feeling began to change.

As I sat there in this group of convicted criminals, I encountered a very powerful but unlikely truth to find in a maximum-security prison: people must be vulnerable in order to change. Of course, I am familiar with the fact that vulnerability is a prerequisite for personal change in psychotherapy, but I didn't expect to find it demonstrated so profoundly in a prison.

The Importance of Vulnerability

The central problem for many of the inmates at Angola, and probably all of us, is selfishness. Criminals are selfish. If they want your property, they will take it. If they want to abuse you, they will take advantage of you. If they want your life, they will take that as well. The psychological term for this type of selfishness is narcissism. A narcissistic person believes that "what I want is all that matters and I am only concerned about myself."

The problem with trying to fix narcissism in a punitive environment like prison is that punishment doesn't work. You might think that teaching selfish people a lesson or taking them down a notch would be good for them. But it isn't. It just makes them angry and more likely to abuse others. I think most prisons have shown this quite clearly. The reason punishment doesn't work in fixing narcissism is that the underlying cause of narcissism is actually shame. Narcissists don't act like they carry any shame, but they do—so treating someone who is narcissistic with punishment and disrespect only shames them more. As one psychologist puts it, "Shame is the cause, not the cure."[5]

I think it is important to point out that everyone has to deal with shame.[6] It's universal. Shame is the fear of not being enough, which results in the fear of humiliation and rejection. It is a matter of degree, of course, but we all have doubts about our self-worth, and so we all have to deal with shame and selfishness in our lives. I didn't want to give the impression that only prison inmates struggle with narcissism and shame because, unfortunately, that's just not true.

The cure for narcissism is empathy, and the only way to learn empathy is through vulnerability. Psychologists have found that almost no one wants to be vulnerable, but almost everyone respects others for being vulnerable. We risk getting hurt when we are vulnerable, but when we witness it in others, we recognize that they are better people for having the courage to do it. A person has to take a risk to change, and vulnerability is that risk.

Empathy is understanding others in a way that connects us to them, and vulnerability is the pathway to that connection. Vulnerability is not just being open; it is the feeling of uncertainty that comes with taking the risk of exposing ourselves emotionally to others. If you are not taking a risk of getting hurt, then you are not really being vulnerable. As I sat in there witnessing the incredible vulnerability of these physically imposing and previously violent men, I was moved. Every one of them would have viewed vulnerability as a weakness in their prior lives, but their capacity for it now was a testimony to the fact that vulnerability leads to change. I did not expect to find this degree of vulnerability in a group of inmates, but they certainly made it clear to me that anyone who truly wants to change must have the courage to be vulnerable, too.

The more I felt these inmates being vulnerable with me, the more I trusted them. You have to be vulnerable in order to trust, and you have to trust in order to be vulnerable—they are two sides of the same coin. Even though their past behavior gave me every reason to feel unsafe, their present vulnerability overpowered my apprehension. The people I work with in therapy often ask me, after a painful divorce or a major betrayal, "How will I ever trust again?" Here's the answer: find someone who is willing to be vulnerable with you, so you can be just as vulnerable with that person—because mutual vulnerability creates trust. It is a risky road to go down, but it is the only way out of the fear of never trusting again.

The last inmate to join us in our meeting that day was George. He came late to the meeting, as he had been involved in mentoring other inmates that morning and couldn't get away. Everyone has a job at Angola; Cain believes that meaningful employment is a part of rehabilitation, and George is a good example. George is responsible for coordinating a program that partners long-term inmates with short-term ones brought in from other prisons. The aim of the program is to provide short-termers with the life skills necessary to make it in the outside world once they are released. George believes strongly in the process of rehabilitation, and it's no wonder. The recidivism rate of Angola's mentoring program is one of the best in the nation. George is doing meaningful work at Angola, and he is grateful for the opportunity to do it. But his life was not always filled with gratitude.

George's Story

George was born and raised in a rough neighborhood in New Orleans. His family became hardened from the widespread drugs and violence that had become a way of life there. He shared with me one incident in which his mother forced him, as a young boy, to fight viciously with another kid until eleven o'clock at night before she would allow him to come inside the family home. She said it was to prove a point.

George lost his father when he was six years old, and he was left to figure out on his own what it meant to be a man. He was mad at the world and looking for trouble every day of his life, so fighting became second nature for George.

"When you argued, you picked up a stick. Or a gun, if you had one," he told me.

Growing up on the streets, fighting at school, and then getting kicked out was just a way of life for George. His mother left when he was fourteen, so he learned how to tell the social workers what they wanted to hear in order to keep them far away from his real life of selling narcotics.

George's older brother joined the New Orleans Police Department and became the only figure in his life he looked up to. Even though he received commendations for his work as a police officer, he had still been raised in the same environment of drugs and violence that George came from. This meant that by day, George's brother carried a gun to enforce the law, but by night, he carried a gun to enforce his drug deals behind closed doors. After their mother left, George moved in with his brother and went into partnership with him selling narcotics. Who better to have an illegal drug business with than a decorated New Orleans police officer?

Unfortunately, these types of business arrangements never end well. When George was sixteen, a rival drug dealer burglarized their apartment, threatening both George's and his brother's lives. They only knew of one thing to do—retaliate. So they did, killing one of the rival drug dealers, for which both of them were convicted of first-degree murder. Today, George and his brother are both serving life sentences at Angola.

Because he was too young to be sent to Angola when he was sentenced, George was first incarcerated at the Orleans Parish Prison. In George's words, "To survive at the Orleans Parish Prison, you needed to have a knife and a big chip on your shoulder."

George was trapped in the cycle of selfishness, punishment, shame, and more selfishness. Every single day he wondered whether was going to survive, so self-preservation kicked in. He was just as violent as the next prisoner—because he had to be.

"I cried out to God for help," he said, but his surroundings were against him. "I couldn't change in that environment."

Through the sheer determination to survive, George lived long enough to eventually be sent to Angola when he turned twenty. From the moment he arrived, he was stunned by how different this place was. He didn't have to carry a knife, and the chip on his shoulder soon became dead weight that was only going to slow him down. George arrived at Angola a selfish and lonely young man with no education or life skills to help him be any different than he had always been. But George could not have imagined the kind of people he was just about to encounter, and the change they would bring about in his life. In his own words: "When I came to Angola I was looking for trouble, but what I found were deeply spiritual men," he said. "These were very positive people who encouraged me to get educated, start reading, and learn to become the positive person that I am today."

The first group of inmates that took an interest in George was a group of practicing Muslims. George gravitated toward them because of the peaceful and respectful way they treated each other. Gradually he realized they had an agenda for George, but it was one that was very unfamiliar to him: they wanted him to be a better man. One member of the group, a man named Johnny Southpaw, offered to teach George how to play chess.

"You can learn a lot about life from the game of chess," Johnny told him. "The people who have an advantage in life are the ones who think, take their time, and use thoughtful strategies to solve their problems."

"I did learn a lot about life through the game of chess," George told me. "But the thing I remember most was when Johnny said, 'I don't care if you ever become a Muslim, or a Christian or a Buddhist. I just care that you become a moral person.'

"I began to see the need to be respectful of other people and that living in relationships with others was what really mattered. My life was in total disarray and I didn't know it until that moment."

There is a lot in the news about violent Muslim extremists in the world, but the Muslims at Angola are nothing like this small percentage of Islamists in the outside world. Their chaplain is peace loving and preaches regularly about social responsibility at the interfaith chapel. They teach classes throughout the week on Islamic beliefs, and they coexist in harmony with the Protestant and Catholic churches there. At one point in my stay at the prison, the warden and I entered one of the chapels to find three inmates, one black and two white, coming out of the back room. They eagerly greeted us in a warm manner and introduced themselves as the Muslim, Catholic, and Protestant ministers of that particular chapel.

I chuckled slightly and asked, "Really? Do you guys ever talk about the differences between what you believe?"

"Oh, sure," the Protestant minister responded. "We know that I'm more exclusive in my beliefs than the Muslim minister, but that doesn't matter here. We were all friends for years long before we ever became ministers."

I almost blurted out "You're kidding!" The minister's calm display of compassion and respect was striking. I couldn't help thinking in that moment that the outside world could learn something about the peaceful coexistence of religions from these inmates. Can Muslims peacefully live alongside Christians and really respect them and get along? They do at Angola. Warden Cain told me later that he would set up a Jewish temple if he could, but you apparently need at least ten members to do so, and he didn't have that many Jewish inmates.

I came to see that Warden Cain's approach to the people at Angola is similar to the way Jesus approached people in need in his day. Take, for example, the miracle of healing the ten lepers (Luke 17:11–19). Jesus healed them because they needed healing; it was simply a divine act of compassion. The only faith he required of them was to "Go, show yourselves to the priests"—the leaders of their own religion—rather than to make a profession of faith in him a condition for their healing. It is true that he was disappointed when only one of them came back interested in a relationship with him, but he allowed all of them to decide for themselves whether, and when, they wanted that. He didn't force it on them; that's just not the way he approached people.

It's no secret at Angola that Burl Cain is a religious man.

But he chooses to have compassion on each inmate right where they are, regardless of whether they share his faith. He has created a place where people can be healed morally and physically, regardless of their belief system. Even if he, too, longs to have them come back to find out more about the religion that motivates him, he doesn't force it on them—just like Jesus. After being healed, the one leper who came back asking for a deeper relationship with Jesus was a Samaritan: the social outcast of their society and the one against whom everyone in that culture held racial prejudices—just like George.

Armed with these new experiences of respectful relationships, George began to evaluate his life. His twenty previous years of violence and bitterness did not go away easily; but his worldview was being challenged, and he didn't really know how to respond. Then, three years after coming to Angola, George experienced a life-changing event. He got into an altercation with another inmate and consequently was put into a restrictive cell. He felt he was being unfairly punished, as the other prisoner had attacked him first, and he was trying to defend himself. But violence at Angola is not tolerated, and the punishment for engaging in violence is often severe. George knew that, so he was afraid of what would happen next. He learned later that the other inmate was removed from the general population as punishment for his part in the conflict.

Frightened and confused, George felt like he was in a dungeon. Up until now, he felt his life had been meaningless. The culture of drugs and violence in which he had been raised had done nothing for him but land him in a maximum-security prison for the rest of his life. What was the point of living? Where was God—if God even existed? Once again, George cried out to God for help. He had heard from some of the other inmates about turning your life over to God, but he had no idea what this meant. He was impressed by the positive attitudes of the people he saw around him, and he knew by comparing himself to them that he needed to change. Now, for the first time in his life, George had the sense that God had put him in this cell to get his complete attention. So, out of desperation, George prayed: "God, if you are real, then give me a Bible."

I don't believe George knew why he selected this particular method of proving God's existence, but in less than ten minutes, someone came up to his cell and said, "Hey, do you need this?"

It was a Bible. George broke down and cried like a baby. He had never felt safe enough to cry so hard and vulnerably before. There was something different about this place. The inmates at Angola were vulnerable in ways he had never seen before, and this made it safe enough for George to be vulnerable himself—and, for the first time, truly vulnerable with God. In that moment, George was convinced that God was real, and he has never doubted it since then. He now felt he had direction in his life. The next day George was released from his cell, after the security videotapes revealed that the incident that had put him there was not his fault. As George put it, "I got saved, and the other guy got shipped out."

George was a new man. He enrolled in the prison's education program and got his GED. With this new thirst for learning, he went on to graduate with an accredited college degree. In 2007 he became an assistant minister in one of the congregations in the prison, and in 2011 he was ordained as head pastor of his own congregation—in addition to his work as the head of the mentoring program at Angola. George had been raised to be a part of the problem, but in coming to Angola he learned how to be a part of the solution. Before Angola, he had never been taught the value of education or given the skills for conflict resolution. Now he teaches other inmates how to resolve conflicts, educate themselves, get and keep employment, and provide a better life for themselves and their families. Having been raised without any good male role models, George has dedicated his life to being one for anyone in Angola who will receive it.

Assistant Warden Fontenot set up a program allowing inmates from other prisons serving sentences of less than ten years to come to Angola for the mentoring program that George heads. They eat, sleep, work, and play sports with prisoners who will never go home, and not a single one of them has ever been harmed or disrespected in any way. After they leave, they can call back to Angola to get advice from their mentors if they get into trouble, whether it's a jam at work or problems in a relationship. Freemen (their term for people living out in the free society) calling inmates at a maximum-security prison for advice. This is nothing short of amazing.

"The real problem for guys trying to go back into society after they leave prison is that they don't have any mentors," George explained. "We are doing something about that."

This program is psychologically profound on several levels. It provides critically needed mentoring for men with limited life skills and very little community support to give them a chance to succeed in the outside world, but it also provides a meaningful life for the inmates at Angola who will never leave. People need to feel productive, and serving as a mentor to someone who has never had one (and probably wouldn't survive in civilized society without one) gives profound meaning to lives of the mentors at Angola who desperately wish someone had done something similar for them.

This illustrates another well-proven psychological principle for personal change that is going on at Angola: mentoring changes people.[7] Psychologists have known for decades that mentoring plays a critical role in a person's success as well as their happiness in life. We now know that having a good mentor is just as important as having a good parent if you want to be a successful person.

In many cultures around the world, rites of passage help young people transition from looking toward their parents for guidance in childhood to looking toward a community of mentors for identity in adult life. Those who successfully make that transition do better in both their personal and professional lives. However, if you have not had a very good relationship with one of your parents, you may not know how to transition to a good mentoring relationship. Many mentoring relationships fail because unresolved parental conflicts are carried over into the adult mentoring relationships, causing them to end unsatisfactorily or never get off the ground in the first place. As you are reading these words, now would be a good time to ask yourself whether you have a strong mentor in your life. If not, ask yourself whether you have some unfinished business with a parent that might be getting in your way.

Trying to live your life as the Lone Ranger doesn't work very well. Psychologists believe the unmet need for mentoring drives young people into gangs, and the isolation that many feel in society is damaging for all of us. Neuropsychologists tell us we are hardwired for connection, and if we do not get the direction and support we need from a mentoring figure, we will likely turn to dysfunctional solutions to our problems. You were not designed to do well on your own. Having the wisdom to seek direction from a mentor just makes good sense.

When the short-termers arrive at Angola, George walks up to them, shakes their hands, and introduces himself to them. He starts building relationships with them right when they arrive because he knows it works. Every time an inmate gets up to speak at their daily motivational meeting, he is instructed to address the group with "Good morning, family." George does this because he knows that most of them have never really felt a part of a family before—at least, not in a good way. He hopes to change that.

He explains to the group, "In my family, we don't steal. In my family, we don't fight. In my family, we take care of each other. In my family, we respect each other. In my family, we love each other."

The way George sees it, the prison is like a family, and Warden Cain is like everyone's father. When you are good, you can expect to be rewarded for your behavior. When you are bad, you can expect to receive the consequences for bad behavior. The difference is that in this family, unlike what most of them experienced before prison, the consequences for bad behavior do not involve being killed. Instead, you serve your time until you get the opportunity to be restored to the family. People fail sometimes, but they have the opportunity to get back up on their feet again. This gives them hope, and this type of family atmosphere is conducive to change. I am happy to report that just as I was making the final changes on this chapter I learned that George will be granted parole at the same time this book will be released into print. People can change for good, and George has convincingly demonstrated that to all who know him.

So, can people really change? Absolutely—even in the worst of circumstances. If you think that you can't change, remember George. Whatever your circumstances, remember they could be worse. And no matter what you have done, or where you are, it is possible to change. The inmates at the Louisiana State Penitentiary are proof of it.

2

Are Some People Just Bad Apples?

Nearly every college student in every introductory psychology class has read about the Stanford Prison Experiment, one of the most famous psychology experiments ever conducted. In 1970, Stanford University professor Dr. Philip Zimbardo set out to identify the personality characteristics of the people who were so bad we had to lock them up in prisons. If we could scientifically identify the characteristics of these people, then perhaps we could identify all the bad people in society before they committed bad acts and prevent much of the social ills in the world today. Zimbardo wanted to identify the bad apples in society before they could spoil the barrel.

Zimbardo randomly assigned college-age men to roles as either prisoners or guards in what was to be a two-week experiment on prisoner behavior in the basement of Stanford's psychology department. He attempted to replicate a typical prison setting and then let the students assimilate into their roles. At first, no one wanted to be guards. They all could imagine needing to know what it was like to be a prisoner at some point in their lives, in case, perchance, they were ever arrested for driving under the influence, evading the draft, or protesting an unjust war. None of them could imagine themselves as guards, a role that didn't fit into their post-graduation career plans.

To make the simulation as real as possible, Zimbardo had the mock prisoners arrested at their homes by the local police, handcuffed, and brought to the simulated prison in police cars. There, they were stripped, deloused, and given hospital gowns (to mimic prison jumpsuits), and they had stockings put on their heads to feign the shaving of their hair. The guards received uniforms and basic instructions on how to conduct themselves from Zimbardo and his expert consultant, Carlo Prescott, who had been released from San Quentin State Prison six months earlier after being incarcerated for seventeen years. Prescott and Zimbardo had just finished teaching a course on prisons, which had inspired the experiment and informed how they conceptualized prison environments. They didn't give the guards a great deal of specific training, as their primary interest was on prisoner behavior. This would turn out to be an extremely significant oversight, as we shall see.

After the first day, none of the guards wanted to be prisoners anymore. They fell immediately into their roles as controlling, demanding, and even abusive jailors. Their behavior became so cruel that half of the prisoners had to be released early due to mental and emotional distress, and the experiment itself had to be terminated after only six days. Even though Zimbardo was present for the entire experiment and saw all of the terrible things that happened as he filmed it from behind a scrim, he was not initially inclined to shut the experiment down. The impetus for the decision came from his girlfriend, Christina Maslach, who confronted him after witnessing the horrendous behavior of the guards for herself. At first, Zimbardo argued with her that this was a scientific experiment and that there was no place for sentimental emotions when conducting objective scientific inquiry, but her tear-filled plea finally stopped him in his tracks: "What you are doing to those boys is a terrible thing!"[1] Zimbardo had set out to identify the psychological characteristics of "bad apples" in the name of science. He never found them—because he was looking in the wrong place.

How could such normal young men have become so bad in such a short time? This is a question that plagued Philip Zimbardo for more than forty-five years, and he devoted extensive scientific exploration to attempt to answer it. In 2007, Zimbardo published *The Lucifer Effect: Understanding How Good People Turn Evil* to explain what he found.[2] Most of us want to explain evil in terms of bad apples. If we believe that evil actions are committed by evil people, then the goal is to identify who they are and avoid them. This is what prisons are for: to put all the bad apples in one place to protect the rest of us from evil. While this notion might be eerily comforting in some way, Zimbardo concluded that, for the vast majority of people, it is not right.

Assuming all evil actions are committed by bad apples is called a *dispositional* view of evil—the view that some people have the disposition to do bad things, and others don't. If you believe this, it makes perfect sense to lock up the evil people in prisons and throw away the key. No more bad apples, no more spoiled barrels. But Zimbardo finally realized that there was another way of thinking about evil that more accurately describes most bad human behavior, which he called the *situational* view. From this perspective, it makes more sense to explain evil actions in terms of the relationships that form us as individuals. Zimbardo's conclusion, after forty-five years of agonizing research on the subject of evil, was that most evil actions can be better explained in terms of bad barrels rather than bad apples, because most people are neither completely good nor completely evil.

Zimbardo set out to identify the personality characteristics of bad people in order to explain why people do bad things. The reason he never found this is because it wasn't the personality characteristics of the people in his study that caused their bad behavior. All of his subjects had gone through psychological tests and examinations before the experiment started, and they were followed for years afterward. There were no outstanding personality characteristics that could explain the bad behavior of the guards, and there was nothing in their subsequent behavior that pointed to any abnormalities either. They were normal college-age men who turned bad in that particular situation—not one of them was an inherently bad apple.

Zimbardo concluded that it is too simplistic to view people as either good or bad. From a psychological perspective, it is best to think of all people as *capable* of both good and evil. There is a complexity to our nature. At times we have an impulse toward good, but in certain situations we have just as strong an impulse toward the bad. There is something within all of us that can recognize goodness, while at the same time we all suffer from selfishness that can cause us to behave very badly. Philosophers and theologians have struggled to explain this for thousands of years. Going all the way back to the apostle Paul in the Bible, we find he wrestled with this when he wrote:

So I find this law at work: Although I want to do good, evil is right there with me. For in my inner being I delight in God's law; but I see another law at work in me, waging war against the law of my mind and making me a prisoner of the law of sin at work within me. What a wretched man I am! Who will rescue me from this body that is subject to death? (Romans 7:21–24)

Paul's basic point is that there is a dichotomy within us as humans that we all have to struggle with, no matter how evolved or spiritual we are. He goes on to say, "So then, I myself in my mind am a slave to God's law, but in my sinful nature a slave to the law of sin" (Romans 7:25). Paul's solution to this dichotomy in our nature is to rely upon a loving God who helps us even though we will continue to struggle with the temptation to do evil things. That is God's life-changing gift to us. But, just as was true for Paul, our ongoing struggle between good and evil will require us to rely on that relationship for guidance and strength for the rest of our lives. The way Paul sees it, this is the "situation" (in Zimbardo's terms) that morally redeems us.

So, from Zimbardo's perspective as well as Paul's, it is not helpful to think there are simply bad apples that are beyond redemption. We could all go in either direction. Granted, there are some dispositional variables that influence our direction, such as mental illness or neurological problems that might result in us classifying some people as truly evil.[3] An example of this, that I explain in more detail later, is that less than 1 percent of the population does not experience guilt, which as you can imagine, produces some truly evil people in our world.[4] But this does not describe the battle between good and evil that most of us struggle with. While there may be some people that do completely give themselves over to evil, the majority of us end up doing good or bad things because of the kinds of relationships we keep. Perhaps the best way to say it is that what is truest about human beings is that we are basically *relational*—our relationships with God and each other will be the most significant factors in determining our moral behavior.

This brings us back to the Stanford Prison Experiment. The most important question is, "How could good people turn so evil in such a short time?" Well, if we think of people as basically relational, then there is one fascinating explanation—because Philip Zimbardo was the warden.

In *The Lucifer Effect*, Zimbardo discloses detailed information about the 1970 experiment with the benefit of decades of research and reflection. He states, regretfully, "I acted like an evil prison administrator, not the good-hearted professor I like to think I am." Zimbardo grew up in a poor area of the South Bronx in New York, which influenced his perspective on officers of the law. He conducted the experiment during a time when it was socially acceptable to reject authority and to, in his words, "oppose the military/industrial establishment." Zimbardo makes several references to the movie *Cool Hand Luke* and how he used the cruel depictions of prison-guard behavior from this movie to inform his attitude about how he set up the experiment. He writes, "I could imagine myself a Paul Newman kind of wisely resistant prisoner, as portrayed in the movie *Cool Hand Luke*. I could never imagine myself as his jailor."

Zimbardo admits he did not spend much time training the guards, because his focus was on prisoner behavior, but this left room for his unofficial perspective to permeate the experiment outside of his conscious awareness. Based upon his consultations with Prescott, Zimbardo gave the guards uniforms, billy clubs, whistles, handcuffs, and mirrored sunglasses exactly like the abusive guards had in *Cool Hand Luke*. He instructed them to create a sense of boredom, loss of individuality, and fear. They were not allowed to physically hurt the prisoners, but they could do everything short of that. Zimbardo referred to the police as "pigs," and when one guard started to act "macho" during the experiment, Zimbardo encouraged him with, "Right on, way to go." Conversely, when he felt one guard was acting too passively toward the prisoners, Zimbardo asked another guard to remind him that he needed to be "more responsive to the job for which he is getting paid." Zimbardo was pleased when the guard gave his fellow participant the further instruction, "We need you to act in a certain way. For the time being, we need you to play the role of the 'tough guard.' We need you to react as you imagine the 'pigs' would." So they did. Within just a few days, the guards were locking the prisoners in closets as solitary confinement, making them urinate and defecate in buckets in their cells, and even forcing some of them to simulate sex acts with each other.

When the prisoners finally rebelled and asked for a meeting with Zimbardo to discuss the deplorable conditions within the mock prison, he agreed to meet with them. But Zimbardo, staying in character as the warden of the prison, donned the mirrored sunglasses himself for the meeting. He later admitted, "I think that perspective came from my lower-class background, which made me identify more with the prisoners than guards." Zimbardo later described himself as "a radical, activist professor," which certainly influenced his perspective on what it meant to be a warden.

Clearly, Zimbardo was not simply an objective scientist conducting a purely scientific study by randomly assigning subjects to controlled experimental conditions. Yes, he was a scientist, but he was also a man being influenced by his own situation. His expert consultant, Carlo Prescott, was so fresh out of his own abusive prison experience that he was "filled with anger about the injustice of the prison system," as Zimbardo wrote. And because both men were from similar lower-class backgrounds, their prejudices toward prison authority were so strong that they not only greatly influenced the design of the prison environment but led Zimbardo and Prescott to tacitly agree that their negative attitudes toward prison guards didn't need to be examined as a possible bias in the study.

So now we have a pretty good answer for how these normal young men became capable of such bad things. First, every single one of us has the capacity to do bad things. That's humbling. But in this situation, the specific relational reason for these young men's bad behavior was the leadership they were under. In other words, leaders change people.

This is a principle of change that has been well researched over the years. Ironically, probably the best-known scientist to study this phenomenon was Zimbardo's childhood friend, Dr. Stanley Milgram. Milgram is the author of another famous psychological experiment that nearly every psychology student reads about in every introductory psychology course.

In Milgram's experiment, conducted at Yale just a few years before Zimbardo's, he had college students participate in what was ostensibly a study on learning. Participating students in one group were told to follow the instructions of the experimenter to see whether we could increase the learning capacities of other students by administering an electric shock each time they got a problem wrong. The intensity of the shock was to be increased after each memory failure to see whether this encouraged them to be more accurate in their subsequent responses. Although the first shocks were relatively mild, the student was to keep increasing the shock up to a point marked *danger* if the learners continued to fail in their responses. In reality, the learners were not actually being shocked; the students administering the "shock" simply heard a recording of someone pretending to be shocked, just to see how far they would go. If they kept going, the learner would cry out at some point, "My heart, my heart! Please let me out!" and then fall silent, leaving the student administering the shock to wonder whether the other person was even still alive. The only motivation for the unaware students to keep going was the experimenter standing next to them in a white lab coat, stating calmly, "You must continue."

Nearly all of us would like to think we'd never go all the way to shocking a person to death. An expert panel of psychiatrists who were asked ahead of time how many people would go to the end said that more than 98 percent of the population would refuse. In reality, however, 65 percent of the participants "shocked" the learners all the way to the level marked as dangerous. And the study has been replicated several times with several different types of people in a number of different places. Shocking, isn't it?

The capacity of normal people to do evil things is stunning. Milgram was trying to understand the horrible acts committed by the Nazis in World War II, so he designed his obedience studies to explore whether or not the Nazis were simply evil people, from a dispositional perspective. What he found, like Zimbardo, was that given the right circumstances, most of us will do evil things simply because we are being told to do them.

Zimbardo and Milgram both grew up in the Bronx; they knew each other in high school and later at Yale. Both were disturbed by the evil perpetrated upon vulnerable people in the world and felt morally compelled to understand why people in positions of authority could act so horribly. Unfortunately, the zeal with which they both went about studying this question ended up damaging the participants in their studies so severely that these and other similar experiments are now considered unethical and barred from scientific study on moral grounds. Even scientists must be prevented from acting badly—because given the right situation, good scientists can do evil things, too.

Philosopher and social commentator Hannah Arendt called this the *banality of evil*. Arendt traveled to Jerusalem to attend the trial of Adolf Eichmann for the war crimes he committed in World War II against the Jewish people. Eichmann had designed and carried out the murder of millions of Jews in a cold and well thought-out plan that he called the Final Solution. His defense? "I was only following orders."

Eichmann was evaluated by six psychiatrists in the hopes of finding a dispositional explanation for his obviously sociopathic behavior. Astonishingly, they all certified him as normal. Arendt, after weeks of testimony, intensive interviews of everyone she could find, as well as extensive research of her own, came to the same conclusion. She found Eichmann to be of average intelligence, of average emotional capacities, and average in just about every other way. In fact, Arendt, like Milgram, concluded that all Nazis were not sociopaths—though most of us would prefer to believe otherwise. Instead, her conclusion was: "The trouble with Eichmann was precisely that so many were like him, and that the many were neither perverted nor sadistic, that they were, and still are, terribly and *terrifyingly normal.*"

Arendt, a brilliant political theorist, went on to write many other important works exposing the abuses of power during the twentieth century. Her commitment to getting at the truth of why people can act so badly was remarkable. But that same commitment to telling the truth cost her dearly. She was Jewish herself, and she was hated for decades by many in the Jewish community for describing Eichmann as normal. Her warning to people then, and to all of us today, was that even very normal people can act in evil ways given the right situation. Or, as she so famously put it, we all should be very aware of the banality of evil.

So trying to identify all people who do bad things as simply bad apples does not seem to be very helpful. For most of us, trying to understand the relational situations in which we act badly seems to be a better approach—Zimbardo's situational view of people. Zimbardo came to admit that, in his role as the warden, he was largely responsible for creating the relational system that caused the students in his experiment to act in such evil ways. In 2007, he wrote, "After we have outlined all the situational features of the Stanford Prison Experiment, we discover that a key question is rarely posed: 'Who or what made it happen that way?' . . . The simple answer in the case of the Stanford Prison Experiment is—me!"

To his credit, Zimbardo recognized that the leader plays a major role as the architect of the situation in which people can behave well or badly. He admitted, "We set an agenda and procedures that encouraged a process of dehumanization and deindividuation that stimulated guards to act in creatively evil ways." This led him to the next logical step in his scientific investigation of human behavior: If bad leaders could create bad people, why couldn't we use good leaders to create good ones? Zimbardo then wondered why we weren't trying to do the opposite of what his friend Milgram had done.

As noted, this reverse-Milgram experiment has never been done. Suppose we actually attempted to perform such an experiment in the laboratory or, better yet, in our homes and communities. Would it work? Could we use the power of authority and of the situation to produce virtue . . . I am confident that we could do a better job of bringing about righteousness in our world.

I find his choice of the word *righteousness* to be very interesting. From a Judeo-Christian perspective, righteousness has always meant *right relationships*—first with God and then with others. Zimbardo was on the right path. But once again, he was not aware of everything he needs to know. He came to see that wardens create bad situations in which bad behavior is generated and has observed this in prisons all over the world. He was unaware of any reverse-Milgram experiments going on anywhere. Consequently, his conclusion in his 2007 book after decades of research on prison systems was this: "My advocacy has largely taken the form of consciousness-raising about the necessity for ending the 'social experiment' of prisons because, as demonstrated by the high rates of recidivism, the experiment has failed." But Zimbardo has never been to Angola.

A Good Barrel

Zimbardo is right in thinking most prisons around the world have failed as social experiments designed to be correctional institutions. But that is only because corrections is not being done correctly; or in most cases, it is not even being attempted. Although he may not know it, his reverse-Milgram experiment is going on in Angola, where people *are* being changed for good.

After the Civil War, the state of Louisiana was heavily populated with newly freed former slaves who possessed little to no education and few resources to support themselves. This climate of desperation led to a rise in crime and the need for a justice system to deal with it. Eventually, the Louisiana Department of Public Safety and Corrections purchased the Angola Plantation, named after the African country where most of the slaves there had originated, to be the site of a new state prison. For years, the prison was itself nothing more than a legalized slave enterprise, working inmates literally to death to produce crops for sale under the guise of punishing them for their misdeeds. Angola was known as the site of modern slavery, and it would come to be known as the Alcatraz of the South and the Bloodiest Prison in America for most of the twentieth century.

But when Burl Cain took over as warden, he came with certain convictions about the inherent worth of each inmate at Angola and a personal calling to do something about improving the conditions there. He believed all people can be changed for good, and he felt responsible for instilling this belief in both the staff and the prisoners under his care. Just as Zimbardo had been mainly responsible for creating the bad barrel at Stanford, Cain felt just as responsible for creating a good one at Angola.

Make no mistake about it: the prisoners who come to Angola are considered bad people by society. Over 90 percent of the prison's inmates will die there while serving life sentences for the crimes they have committed. In its worst years, there were daily fights, regular stabbings, and up to forty murders per year at Angola. Books have been written about this brutal time, movies made, and the stories told are legendary. You might think that trying to change the inmates at Angola through any form of corrections would be hopeless, but that is only if you view them as a bunch of bad apples. Warden Cain didn't.

Unlike Zimbardo, Cain believes that prisons can be reformed into places of rehabilitation and respect. He doesn't believe that these people were sent to Angola to be punished—he believes they were sent there to be changed. His term for this is *moral rehabilitation*. He knew the prisoners came from difficult backgrounds, had done bad things, and had never experienced anything close to a reason to be good. He wanted to create a prison environment that would do exactly that. He wanted to see what would happen if you put a criminal in a good apple barrel. Cain then embarked on a reverse-Milgram experiment unlike anything Zimbardo has ever seen.

Cain knew the only type of rehabilitation that made sense in a prison environment was a moral one. He didn't want to simply make prisoners smarter or more skilled; he wanted to change their moral character. He also knew that, especially in the South, morality is taught in church. Of course, atheists can be moral people, but the church offers a system of teaching morality. So Cain started by bringing in a Bible class from his own church. There was a chapel in the prison, but only a few inmates used it, and the chaplain meant well but had a job that would have been overwhelming for anyone. Cain knew he needed to do something about that.

This led to conversations with the New Orleans Baptist Theological Seminary about setting up an educational branch of the seminary inside the prison at Angola. It was a radical idea, but one that had tremendous potential on many levels. First, it would bring the moral teachings of Christianity into the prison at the highest level. Second, it would offer inmates the opportunity to receive an accredited college education. And third, it would create college-educated ministers who, in turn, could introduce the rest of the prison population to life-changing relationships with a loving God. On top of all this, because the seminary viewed this endeavor as a part of their Christian mission, they would offer these college degrees to the inmates for free—so it wasn't going to cost the taxpayers of the state of Louisiana a penny. Who could object to that?

Because Cain had formerly been a teacher, he knew the value of education. Most of the prisoners sent to Angola were functionally illiterate, which was part of the reason they ended up there. Cain firmly believed that educating people changes them. It opens up their minds to the larger world, and it teaches them problem-solving skills, thoughtful strategies to replace impulsive actions, and the capacity to apply knowledge to life situations—otherwise known as wisdom. Once some inmates started to become educated, others began to turn to them for advice. A college education became attractive to these inmates, and the seminary started to flourish.

To date, Angola has graduated more than two hundred inmates from the seminary with accredited bachelor's degrees in Christian ministry. This qualifies them to be ordained pastors within the prison walls with the same education and skills you would find in pastors of churches on the outside. Cain's project for moral rehabilitation is now functioning at an amazing level. There is a qualified minister in every dorm, eight church buildings built and operated by inmates, and dozens of congregations with inmate pastors preaching sermons on Christian values multiple times each week. You can't go anywhere in the prison today without finding someone who is willing to talk with you about God and good behavior, because college-educated ministers encouraging others to do good are everywhere.

Originally, prisons were created as a place where we could send wrongdoers to punish them until they repented for their misdeeds. The word *penitentiary* comes from *penitent*, or remorseful for what one has done. But Cain's concept of a prison was completely different. He didn't want to simply punish people and make them feel bad; he wanted to create a place where they could actually change. To do this he needed to make Angola safe, so he instituted swift and severe consequences for violence within the prison walls. In most prisons, violence is accepted—or even allowed—by guards who have given up on any hope of rehabilitating inmates. With strict consequences for violence at Angola, however, the word got out quickly that you wanted to think twice before hurting someone. And just as quickly, a sense of safety spread through the prison yard as inmates began to realize they didn't have to always be on guard, they didn't have to carry a knife, and they could sleep through the night without fear of being assaulted in their sleep. The way Cain put it to me was simple: "I have to protect these men." Unlike Zimbardo, Cain had a clear sense of responsibility for the well-being of his prisoners as their warden. Rather than encouraging guards to be more macho, Cain fired them for even swearing at an inmate. His view is that swearing offends a man's pride, which forces him to turn violent as a matter of principle, and Cain feels a moral responsibility to protect his inmates from violence. There are no mirrored sunglasses, no tough-guard role models, and no macho attitudes allowed. A good barrel is most importantly a safe one. Because Warden Cain is a good leader, he understands a critically important element in facilitating change among the inmates: people need to feel safe in order to change.

Facing Danger Honestly

People come to me for help as a psychologist because they want to change; at least they say they do. Then I begin the process of psychotherapy, which for the most part is dedicated to dealing with their resistance to change. It may sound contradictory, but the bulk of psychotherapy is devoted to resistance analysis—or, put more simply, getting people to see how they are fighting me as I try to help them change.

Originally, psychologists thought we had to break through our clients' resistances and confront them on their dysfunctional behavior, and unfortunately, most people still come to me with a similar attitude to this today. They say, "Look, just tell me what to do, and I'll change." This sounds nice, but it rarely works.

Psychologists have come to understand that all people resist change because they are afraid, and the things they do to defend themselves cannot be easily surrendered. My role, then, is not to confront people for resisting change but to help them see why they *must* resist it based upon what they have learned in life up to this point. People resist change because they feel they are in danger, and they can't do anything different until they feel safe. Resistance analysis then becomes, in effect, danger analysis. Rather than forcing people to open up to me who won't, I help them see why opening up to people has never paid off for them before, so it's understandable for them to question why they would do it with me now. As they come to see that I understand how dangerous opening up has been to them, paradoxically they feel more secure. Promising people that therapy is safe doesn't work; recognizing that therapy is not safe does. People feel safe when someone honestly recognizes the danger around them. Ignoring it or telling them they shouldn't be afraid of it only causes them to resist change. People need to feel safe in order to change, and honestly facing how dangerous life is lays the foundation for it.

Warden Cain's common-sense approach to violence is nothing short of inspired. If you reward good behavior and have swift consequences for dangerous behavior, you create an environment where people feel safe. Then the world makes sense to the people who live in it. Rather than claiming that violence is just something we have to accept in prison, Cain established it as something not tolerated in Angola. This honest recognition of danger is necessary in order for people to feel safe enough to change.

Opportunities for Change

With a secure sense that the warden will protect them from violence, the inmates of Angola have come to view him as a loving but firm father figure, which almost none of them had before. Cain often says, "I will be as good as you let me and as mean as you make me." He loves to reward good behavior and is quick to set consequences for the bad. As I walked around the main prison yard with Cain and his assistant, I was impressed by the freedom that each inmate felt to be able to approach him and speak to him personally. Occasionally someone would bring up a pressing concern, and Cain would address it on the spot. If the inmate had demonstrated good behavior for a long enough period of time, he would adjudicate the matter immediately and agree to the inmate's request.

Cain chose to relate to the inmates as an "askable" leader, rather than granting them an audience with a distant authority figure behind mirrored sunglasses. I witnessed firsthand the powerful impact of each personal conversation an inmate had with a warden who took their concerns seriously and responded to them with fairness and respect. Everyone knew him to be a strong authority figure, but they were all just as certain he would listen empathically to their needs. In this way, Cain has created a community built on a sense of safety, with inmates who know they can improve their station in life based upon reasonable rewards and consequences for their behavior. It is up to them to decide what they want to make of themselves; it isn't the warden or the guards punitively holding them back.

There are many ways to improve your life at Angola. You may never get out, but you can make a better life while you are there. Cain knows that doing meaningful work leads to a sense that your day has been worthwhile, and over time, you feel worthwhile yourself. Most prisoners start off working the fields when they come to Angola. Its eighteen thousand acres surrounded by the Mississippi River are home to some of the richest soil in the South, making it an ideal agricultural environment. The inmates feed themselves out of the four million pounds of vegetable crops they produce each year and the two thousand head of cattle they raise. "We never open a can," as Cain says proudly. But working in the fields is just a starting place—an opportunity to demonstrate with good behavior your desire for advancement.

If all goes well, inmates can move on to a job in one of Angola's manufacturing facilities making mattresses and brooms, or working in one of the print shops, or silk screening, tractor repair, making license plates, or working in transportation. There is also an opportunity to work on the award-winning magazine, the *Angolite*, or at the television or radio station. There are other opportunities to work in the prisoner-run hospice program or mentor program, to participate in musical groups, and to create your own line of crafts that you can sell at annual events for the public. And then there is the world-famous Angola Prisoner Rodeo.

The Angola Rodeo

Each Sunday in October, some fifteen thousand freepeople from all over the world show up at the Louisiana State Penitentiary to witness the prisoner rodeo. In an arena built just for this event, outsiders easily walk among hundreds of inmates as they shop for handcrafted items that the prisoners have spent all year creating to sell. These range from belts, purses, and furniture to meticulously fashioned model ships that represent hundreds of hours of expert craftsmanship. Seventy thousand visitors spend more than $500,000 each year at the event, allowing the rodeo to be self-sustaining without costing taxpayers anything at all.

But the fair and craft booths are just the prelude to the

Angola Rodeo. Fifteen thousand visitors all pack into the circular arena to cheer on the amazing acts of cowboy skill put on by the prisoners themselves. Expert consultants are brought in to ensure that things are done correctly, but all the talent in the events is supplied by the inmates. There is roping, racing, bucking broncos, bull riding, and daring events of all kinds. My first trip to Angola was to attend the rodeo, and it was just as breathtaking as any other rodeo I had ever seen (and I've been to my fair share). As you are probably thinking, it is also dangerous.

Sometimes inmates do get hurt, just as in any other rodeo. Of course, as in other rodeos there are medical staff and ambulances on hand ready to respond to injuries. Some have criticized the decision to host such a dangerous event at a prison. Because the inmates are a captive population, some feel that risky events of this nature should not be allowed, and others have pointed to the racial disparity of the inmates because 75 percent of them are black.[5] But after multiple conversations with several of the wardens, many of the staff, and dozens of inmates, I have come to a different conclusion. For the prisoners who volunteer to participate in the rodeo, it's a chance to be a hero for a day.

In addition to those concerned for the well-being of the prisoners, some family members of the victims of the crimes committed by the inmates at Angola have expressed their displeasure at allowing them to participate in the rodeo. While I understand they are still suffering, I would like to explain why the rodeo is an important part of the moral rehabilitation going on at Angola. The Angola Rodeo is an internationally famous event. Family members, neighbors, and news media come from all over to participate. The prisoners who compete in the events volunteer for the privilege, and they must have an excellent and long-standing behavior record before they are even eligible. Obviously, this motivates them to take responsibility for their behavior throughout the year, in keeping with Cain's philosophy of offering rewards for good behavior to inspire personal responsibility.

Most of these inmates live lives of isolation away from their families, and if they do have contact with them they struggle with deep feelings of shame as they look back over their lives and the impact their incarceration has on their loved ones. What is even sadder is that once many of these prisoners enter the walls of Angola, they are as good as dead to their families and now forgotten. Eighty percent of these inmates never get a visitor—ever. And when some of them die, no one even comes to claim the body.

Feeling insignificant is toxic to people. Much of the violence in the former lives of these inmates grew out of this feeling of insignificance. By contrast, the Angola Rodeo gives them a chance to do something, once a year, that results in public applause—a chance to reverse their feelings of failure and shame. Yes, the rodeo events are physically dangerous, but facing physical danger is one of the few challenges the inmates of Angola feel they can face better than most. It's a chance to be a man of courage in one of the only ways they know how, and for a brief moment not feel ashamed of who they are now. This doesn't excuse what they have done in the past, but it's a chance to show to themselves and everyone there that they care about what others think of them. They want a place in society, even if they will never rejoin it on the outside, and they don't want to have to look down at the ground as they walk away. The inmates of Angola are striving to show that they are no longer bad apples and that they can be good people, ones you might even like to have in your apple barrel if they were ever given the chance to show you how much they have changed.

This illustrates another important principle of change at work at Angola, one that is directed at the shame and insignificance that almost every one of these inmates felt before they came here: feeling significant changes people. We all have a deep longing within us to be seen as worthwhile. We cannot live meaningful lives without it. We all long to know and be known, and to love and to be loved. Consistently having those needs met changes us for good.

Your Life Matters

The Hawthorne Works electric company just outside Chicago conducted a research project in the 1920s and '30s to help employees improve their work performance. The company commissioned a study to try to determine whether workers would become more productive in higher or lower levels of light, and researchers carefully observed the performance of thousands of workers when they increased or decreased the levels of light surrounding their workstations. The results were very interesting: workers improved their performance each time the light was increased or decreased. It didn't matter which; changing the intensity of the light in either direction improved worker performance.

Unsure what to make of this finding, the researchers then changed the cleanliness of the floors surrounding workstations, and what do you know? Workers' productivity increased. Then they rearranged the workstations themselves, and, again, productivity improved. So then they moved the workstations to entirely new locations, changed break times, and shortened or lengthened the workday. In each and every case, productivity improved. In the end, the researchers found that everything they did resulted in an improvement in work performance. Then the "light" came on for the researchers themselves. Changing the environment wasn't making the workers improve—paying attention to them was. Each time something changed in the work environment, the workers knew someone was watching them and interested in their performance. This made them feel significant, and feeling significant changes people. Researchers everywhere now call this the Hawthorne effect.

We all want to matter. It is hardwired within us to want to feel seen and recognized as having worth. If someone is paying attention to us, we feel significant, and we start to believe that we matter. Feeling significant makes us come alive.

If we feel insignificant to others, on the other hand, we lose the motivation to want to improve. If this goes on long enough, we become bitter and stop caring about improving our lives and behavior. This is extremely toxic to the human soul—and it's at the root of why most of the inmates at Angola ended up there. They felt that everyone had stopped caring about them, so they stopped caring about everyone else. Most of the inmates at Angola came to believe they would never live a long life, so they stopped caring about their own futures as well as everyone else's. Feeling insignificant keeps people stuck.

Warden Cain made it his mission to change how the inmates of Angola felt about themselves. He knew that selfish people could become moral people, and he believed that creating an atmosphere in which they could feel significant was essential to making that transformation possible. Cain believed that giving the inmates of Angola a chance to be a hero for a day was important because he knew that feeling significant changes people.

As Warden Cain puts it, "It's simple. Criminals are selfish people, and the opposite of that is a moral person. To participate in the rodeo you have to demonstrate that you can be a moral person, one who cares about what others feel and one that won't hurt you. If you are a changed person, then prove it." And that is precisely what the inmates at Angola are doing. When the thousands of freepeople attend the rodeo each October, mixing in among the hundreds of inmates who have earned the privilege to participate, there are no incidents of violence at all, and there have only been rare occurrences of misbehavior of any kind.

It might be hard for the victims' families to think of the prisoners at Angola ever being praised. But that is partly because we tend to think of evil as coming from bad apples. What these prisoners did was wrong; they wouldn't be at Angola otherwise. But isn't it in the best interest of everyone in society to help them change if they can? None of us benefits from believing that all evil only comes from inherently bad apples and that bad people can't change. If you take bad apples and put them in good barrels, amazing things can happen. Some never change, it's true. But given just the right barrel, some do.

People Are Hardwired to Follow Authority

If there is one thing Stanley Milgram, Philip Zimbardo, and Burl Cain have all demonstrated for us, it's that the architect of your barrel is extremely important. The leaders you follow play a crucial role in your moral character. You may think you would never act in the immoral ways that the inmates at Angola did in their previous lives, but that's what the subjects of the Yale and Stanford experiments thought before participating in them. Good people can do bad things if they follow the wrong leaders.

Zimbardo didn't mean to do it, but he set up a situation in which very normal young men acted in evil ways because he led them down the path to do it. Just because everyone around you is following the leader doesn't make it the right direction to go. Often in life, following the morally better path is not the most popular way to go.[6]

On the other hand, Warden Cain is a perfect example of what psychologists call primal leadership, which is "not domination, but the art of persuading people to work toward a common goal."[7] Good leaders have learned their primary task is to inspire others to *want* to follow, which creates a culture that is open and produces change in people's character far beyond what any authoritarian leader could achieve. This is the difference between control and authority. Control is the power to make others do what you want; authority is the power to inspire them to want what you want. Both are persuasive forms of power, but a good leader knows how to lead with authority.

Renowned business consultant Robert Greenleaf has another term for primal leadership: servant leadership.[8] The task of a servant leader is to inspire others from within their hearts rather than dominating them by lording power over their heads. If you ever doubt the effectiveness of this leadership style, just remember that Warden Cain has demonstrated at the largest maximum-security prison in America that people are hardwired to follow authority.

Stanley Milgram effectively demonstrated the human need to follow authority, but is this something we learn or are we born that way? Psychologists decided to study this in six-month-old babies, who are known to have a fear of heights as soon as they are able to crawl.[9] In one experiment, they placed infants on a Plexiglas table, but they designed the table with an optical illustration: there appeared to be a drop-off of several feet halfway to the real edge of the tabletop.[10] Placing the babies on the obviously secure end of this Plexiglas table, they instructed their mothers to vary their facial expressions as they waited at the other end of what appeared to be a very deep drop. When the mothers expressed fear on their faces, none of the babies would venture off the apparent cliff. When the mothers smiled, all but three babies scampered right across. The researchers' conclusion was that humans are hardwired almost from birth to follow the emotional direction of authority figures, even if it means plunging to our deaths. As it turns out, self-preservation does not appear to be the strongest human motivation in all situations, because there are times when the need to follow a trusted authority overrides it.

So are some people just bad apples? We must admit that a very small number of people are committed to evil acts and will hurt others without a conscience, and despite all our best efforts to help them, they never change. Warden Cain calls them predators, and we know that they do exist. But there are many people we send to prison who are not bad apples. Those are the people who are not completely evil, but have somehow gotten lost. They have followed the wrong leaders, felt continually unsafe, lived lives of tortured insignificance, and failed to find an authority figure they could trust even though they have longed for it since the moment they could crawl. According to Professor Zimbardo and Warden Cain, this describes most of the people who do bad things, and these people aren't intrinsically bad apples—because they can change. This is good news for all of us, because if they can change, so can you.

3

How to Become a Person of Character

"You have to meet Carolina," Warden Cain said with a strange smile on his face. He was particularly excited about the prospect of me meeting this inmate while I was at the prison. Clearly, he was eager for me to witness the moral rehabilitation going on at Angola firsthand. He relished showing outsiders what was happening within the walls of this maximum-security prison; now he wanted to do this for me.

"This guy was a human animal," Cain said with a peculiar enthusiasm in his voice. "I can't think of anyone who has changed more than Carolina. You have to see this for yourself."

So off we went to the main prison to meet the inmate nicknamed for his roots in rural South Carolina. As he was escorted into the private room where we were to have our conversation, his wide frame and acne-scarred complexion communicated strength and rugged authenticity. He seemed friendly enough as he shook my hand, but even though there were only three of us there, Carolina seemed to fill the room with his presence.

Warden Cain and Carolina talked for a bit, discussing Carolina's recent trip to a neighboring prison and the possibility of him traveling to another prison in the near future. They seemed to disagree about whether this was a good idea, and I was surprised by the directness with which Carolina addressed the warden. Their exchange had more of the feeling of two colleagues processing a business decision than a warden telling a prisoner what to do. *Man, this guy is sure of himself,* I thought. Their conversation ended with strong positive feelings communicated between the two, with the final decision left clearly in the warden's hands—and then Warden Cain politely left the room.

At first, Carolina didn't say much. He looked me squarely in the eyes and just listened as I explained why I was there and what I would like to hear from him. Even while he was silent, the intensity of Carolina's personality made me a bit nervous. He wasn't talking, but his focused gaze and confident posture were communicating a palpable strength. While I calmly told him about my interest in the lives of the inmates at Angola and my desire to tell their stories to others, I couldn't help thinking about the fact that this man was serving a life sentence for murder. The warden's description of Carolina had left me with the suspicion that he had taken more than one life. And here I was alone in a room with him, about to ask him probing personal questions that some people might find threatening or possibly even offensively intrusive. What if this didn't go well? No doubt, I thought, this man has a long history of poor impulse control. I couldn't help asking myself once again, *Is this really such a good idea?*

"There are two types of prisoners," Carolina began. "Predators and prey. And both of them are easily identified. The first thing prisoners try to identify is whether or not you are afraid. A fearful man puts off different body movements—they look at the floor, or shuffle their feet, or if somebody asks them a question and they don't know how to respond, well, this draws the predator to you. When I go into a prison, I exhibit certain behaviors to identify the type of man that I am. I make eye contact, and I establish that I don't want your trouble but I'm not going to back down from it, either."

This division of people into predators and prey is rather explicit, but it's really not that different from that the way many outside the prison walls think about power in relationships. Both predators and prey view vulnerability as a weakness, believing you have to look out for yourself and never give up your power to anyone else willingly. People who think this way view dominance as the only real form of power: you either control others or are controlled by them. Those are the only two options. People who think this way tend to fear depending upon others and never get at the root of why they are the way they are. Neither predators nor prey ever change, because *viewing people as victims keeps everyone from changing*. It doesn't matter if you believe the other person is powerless or if you believe you are—the belief that anyone is powerless keeps everyone stuck. Anyone can be victimized by abuse, but *victims* are people who believe they are powerless and get caught up in fear-based relationships with perpetrators who agree with them.

Even though both people in these types of relationships view dominance as power, they are not really driven by the thrill of control or the threat of being controlled; they are driven by the fear of exposing their own shame. This is just as true of the predators, who violate others because of their own self-loathing shame, as it is of their victims, who believe they are powerless because of theirs. No one can get free from this pattern of abuse until they see that their own shame is at the root of their power struggles. The kind of power that changes people is not about domination but about inspiration that comes from an authoritative relationship that instills confidence, love, and self-discipline. People who view power as domination are trapped in a life of shame that will never give them true power. But when Carolina went to prison, he wasn't thinking at all about the origins of his predatory behavior. He was just trying to stay alive.

"I first came to Angola in the early '80s," he told me. "It was quite different then. It was violent, and not just because everyone expected prisoners to be violent—it was actually accepted that this is just the way things are in prison. You had freepeople jumping on inmates and inmates jumping on freepeople, it didn't make any difference if you were wearing a uniform or not. I mean if an inmate wanted to fight a security officer, 95 percent of the time he would get it."

"You lived in a place where prisoners were stabbing each other on a regular basis. You couldn't walk around and not have respect. You had to have that. Men died here. Inmate-on-inmate killing was a very common occurrence. I've witnessed quite a few prisoners lose their lives senselessly over inconsequential things."

He had my full attention. I wondered whether he had only witnessed this senseless loss of life in Angola or had perhaps participated in it as well.

I went on to learn that Carolina had been in four prisons in three states, but that he was to spend the rest of his life here at Angola. His history of institutional living started at the age of nine, when he was committed to a mental institution in South Carolina. He was supposedly there for evaluation. He had been violent and rebellious for years, and, in his words, "They had to figure out what's wrong with this kid." If his father told him he had to do his homework, he would tear it up and throw it out the school bus window. He couldn't count the number of fights he'd had in every school he attended.

Carolina grew up in an atmosphere of violence. His father was one of the "most feared" men in every place they ever lived, he told me. And his mother was "not to be trifled with" either. His father raised him with the belief that there was only one way to settle a dispute, and that was to be a conqueror. "Losing for me was not an option," he said. "If I lost a fistfight, then I lost two. Because daddy would beat me senseless just for losing."

He described his family as dysfunctional. His father was a good man when he wasn't drinking, but the minute he took a drink, he became entirely different. He was an angry drunk, and so was Carolina's mother. They masked their anger when they were sober and mutually enabled their alcoholism by excusing the violence and abuse in their family as the result of their short tempers or just an anger problem. And, as is true in most alcoholic families, the children were the ones who suffered the most.

Carolina took the brunt of most of his father's rage, which crystalized in him the only two emotions he would know until the age of forty-four: hatred and indifference. He can remember to this day the event that caused him to begin to hate his father. He can still see his mother, pregnant with his little sister, standing in the kitchen arguing with his father, as they often did. His father was driving a beer truck then, and with the easy access to alcohol, his rages and abuse had become more frequent. This time, the arguing went too far. This time, his father didn't stop at yelling and intimidation. This time, he beat Carolina's pregnant mother almost to the point of her death and that of her unborn child. Carolina hated his father for that, and he spent the rest of his life rebelling against him for it. Something snapped in Carolina that day, and the typical rewards and punishments that shape the behavior of normal children no longer worked with him. If he did something right, his father's praise meant nothing to him. And if he did something wrong, punishment only made him hate his father more. The more Carolina was punished, the more he hated. He knew no fear, only hatred and indifference.

Carolina went on to live a life of violence and total disregard for everyone. Because of his natural intelligence, he was able to work a job, buy a house, drive a nice truck, and conduct a lucrative drug business on the side. This last was partially for the money, but mostly for the threat of danger he couldn't live without. He was a white man dealing in an almost exclusively black environment, trying to prove to everyone his dominance. Eventually he, like his father, became the most feared man around, and everyone knew it.

After several incarcerations for lesser crimes, Carolina finally killed a man with an AK-47 in an incident that he knew would put him away for life, especially given his past violent crimes. So he decided to run. Over the next three and a half years, Carolina fled to Mexico, Canada, and distant parts of the United States to escape the law. He knew he was headed to prison for life this time, so he made up his mind that if they caught him, he wouldn't go down without a fight—he was going to take as many of them with him as he could.

As I discussed in the last chapter, self-preservation may not always be the most basic human motivation, but I don't have to tell you that it is a powerful one. When your life is threatened, whether physically or psychologically, you will have a very powerful urge to protect yourself. This defensive activity preserves life and is not necessarily a problem when you are aware of what you are doing. But it is important to recognize that self-preservation at all costs prevents change. Blinking is necessary to protect your eyes at times, but you can't live your life with your eyes closed all the time. If your life is primarily motivated by self-preservation, you will end up lost and alone at the end of it. A self-focused life may allow you to preserve your physical life, but you will fail to find any meaning in that life. Or, as the saying goes, just because you really don't want to die doesn't mean you really want to live.

In order to change, you have to be open to outside influences. Growth happens in the context of connection to others. But in the face of threat, we put up walls to protect ourselves. This self-protection is automatic but only helpful if done for a limited time. The problem isn't that we get defensive once in a while; the problem comes when we get stuck there. This was Carolina's difficulty, and it is one many people share with him. Some people feel threatened most of the time and, as a result, have an almost constant need to be self-protective. Once you are in this mind-set, you cease to be open to growth or change because you can't see past your very immediate fears. The tragedy is that while self-protection is necessary temporarily, it is one of the biggest obstacles to personal change in anyone's life. Self-protection at the expense of your connection to God and others prevents meaningful personal change, and surrendering your grip on self-preservation at all costs is the price you must pay to get it. Carolina was about to discover this truth for the first time in his life.

"How they caught me is that I met the first person in my life that I wouldn't hurt," Carolina confessed. "I didn't know that I loved her at the time; I didn't know what love was. All I knew was that I couldn't get away from my desire to see her laugh, to see her happy, and to just wake up in the morning and see her smile. She had been abused and lived a terrible life before I met her. And now I saw her laugh and giggle all the time."

"I will never forget the moment when I saw my profile come up on the TV as a wanted man. The first thing that entered my mind was that I would have to kill her if she recognized me. That was my natural thought. But when it came right down to it, I couldn't do it. For the first time in my life, I refused to hurt another person. I was so struck by this feeling that I took all my weapons and threw them in Puget Sound. The federal authorities were pretty frustrated with me for that later, but it was the only thing I could think to do. I made a commitment to her right then and there that I would live with her and not hurt another human being, and that if I got caught, I wouldn't resist." And eventually, that is just what happened.

Carolina was finally arrested in 1997 and returned to Angola for good in 1999. As he was waiting to be transferred there, he heard the new warden on the radio talking about how there had not been a single fistfight over the entire Fourth of July weekend. He thought "now, that has to be a lie." Carolina had been to Angola; he knew what a violent place it was. But he was not prepared for what was to happen this time.

As he arrived at the reception center at the prison, Carolina felt something distinctly different about the place. The first time he had been to Angola, there had been a thick sense of oppression that you could cut with a knife as you entered the gates. "You could feel it, like walking into a steam house," he told me. But this time it felt very different. He couldn't identify it at first, but later he described it as a palpable sense that the oppression was gone.

Looking back, Carolina will tell you he didn't function well in free society. There were too many rules and expectations and too much responsibility. Prison turned out to be an environment in which he could function well. So Carolina quickly adjusted back to his prison life. He was a predator—one of the most feared. Returning to this role was only natural for him, and for the next several years, he again lived a life of hatred and indifference. If he hated a man, he would hurt him without a second thought. If he felt indifferent toward someone, he would manipulate situations to entertain himself with the man's misery. Carolina didn't like people, and he didn't care.

Then, in 2007, he came across an event that changed everything. He signed up for a Kairos meeting sponsored by some people from the outside world because he had heard the freepeople's food was pretty good. Kairos is a Christian organization that brings in people to talk to inmates about the life-changing power of a relationship with Jesus Christ. But that's not how Carolina saw it. Just two days before the meeting, another inmate had asked Carolina whether he believed in God.

"Absolutely not," was his characteristically defiant reply. "God is a fairy tale, and anyone who believes in God is a fairy. That's where you find fairies, in fairy tales."

He viewed the people from Kairos as a "bunch of middle-class do-gooders, crying and moaning about a miraculous God that delivered them from a pharmaceutical drug addiction or some alcohol problem or helped them get over their wife running away with the milkman." At the time, there was nothing more disgusting to Carolina than watching a man cry, so he was so repulsed by the meeting that he was about to create a violent scene in order to get out of it when, in his own words, "God just reached down and snatched the hate and indifference out of my heart."

Carolina was in a world of pain. He hated his father, he hated authority, and he hated everyone on the planet, including himself—more than he knew. The arrogance it takes to be a predator does not come from confidence; it comes from the deepest form of shame that destroys a man's soul. He was in such mind-numbing pain that evening that he was just about to explode into a rage when he discovered a profound psychological principle regarding personal growth: pain is an opportunity for change.

One of the oldest diseases on record is leprosy. Those afflicted with it in ancient times became horribly disfigured and were relegated to the outskirts of the village for fear they might be contagious. What people didn't know at the time was that leprosy is a disorder of the nervous system that prevents those who have it from feeling physical pain, and it especially likes to settle in the extremities of the body, such as the fingers, toes, nose, and ears. This means people with leprosy may stub their toes or cut their fingers and not even know it. Consequently, in ancient times, they would regularly get infections and lose parts of their bodies because of a lack of treatment for their injuries. So the actual cause for the disfigurement of leprosy is the inability to feel pain. If you don't know you are hurt, you can't respond with the needed care.

Too many people try to be *emotional* lepers. They believe they should rid themselves of their pain and never admit that they feel it. Pain gives us opportunity to respond to an injury with needed change, so the ability to feel pain and admit it to others is actually a gift. When you are in pain, it means you need to pay attention. Trying to avoid your pain, run away from it, or medicate yourself to escape it is usually a bad idea. Listening to your pain and trying to get at the root of what is causing it is a much better one. Emotional leprosy prevents change, but the ability to respond to pain is the beginning of healing. His entire life, Carolina had been running as fast as he could to avoid his pain. That was all about to change, in an instant.

Just as he was finishing his chocolate chip cookie and preparing to make his dramatic exit, Carolina suddenly lost complete awareness of everything around him. He couldn't see anybody, he couldn't hear anything, and he had no idea what was happening to him. The only thing he was aware of was that he was in pitch blackness and there were no voices in his head. In his forty-four years of life, Carolina had never been without the hate-filled voices in his head instructing him to cheat, to lie, to manipulate, and to hurt others. That's all he knew. And in an instant, that was completely taken from him.

"I don't know how to explain it to you so that it is understandable, but in one moment I was full of the most murderous rage, and in the twinkling of an eye it was all gone," he said. "I felt this overwhelming sense of something that I now know was love. But at the time, I didn't know what love was. I just knew that I didn't hate anybody anymore."

Carolina's response to this event was mixed. He was both at peace and afraid at the same time. He felt a warmth from this new sensation that he was later to identify as love. At first, he said it was as though he was blindfolded and some-one was calling his name; he knew it was his name, but he couldn't identify who it was that was calling him. He didn't believe in God, so thinking in those terms didn't occur to him at the time. At the same time, he was fearful. "How am I going to survive without hatred and indifference?" was the first question that came to mind. Hatred and indiffer-ence were the only allies he had ever had. They had carried him through some of the roughest prisons in the United States. He didn't know what he would do without them.

Carolina was confused, but unmistakably changed. He hadn't prayed to God to ask for this—he was eating a choco-late chip cookie. Nobody at the meeting had told him to do it. He didn't even like Christians; in fact, they were the guys that he preyed upon the most because he viewed them as weak. But Carolina could neither explain nor alter the way he now felt. He didn't hate anymore. For the first time in his life, he was at peace. Quite miraculously, something hap-pened in that moment that left Carolina a changed person.

Reluctantly, at first, he turned to some of the other inmates who were attempting to live spiritual lives to try to make sense out of what was happening. He joined in on some of their groups, started reading the Bible, and even started going to a prison church to listen to a prison pastor. Things evolved, and he eventually came to under-stand his dramatic experience as a divine act by a loving God who had reached down and taken the hatred out of his heart. Carolina now knew what love was, and he knew that a personal experience with a loving God had completely changed him.

While Carolina had little respect for freepeople whining about their first-world problems, he did respect his fellow inmates, who understood his world. Fortunately for him, there were many inmates at Angola who not only knew what it was like to live the violent life he had known but had experienced the transforming power of the love of God. He was able to sort out the inmates who had *prison religion,* or *jailhouse* religion—the term the inmates used to describe insincere religion they didn't trust—from those he described as truly *born again.* And for the first time in his life, Carolina found a caring community of relationships. Finally, he found his home.

"Remember when we first sat down?" Carolina said to me. "I didn't ask you if you were born again or a Christian. I told you that you were born again, because I knew it. When you come into a man's presence you have to ask yourself, *How do you feel?* That's how you know if he has a personal relationship with God. That's how a man knows whose voice it is that is calling his name—relationship. Otherwise you might hear the voice but you won't know who it is that is calling you."

Carolina went on to describe how, just like in the outside world, some of the people who called themselves Christians there were predators simply cloaking themselves in religious appearances. He is highly perceptive and relies heavily on his emotional intuition in sorting out true believers from what psychologists call *false selves.* He is fully aware that some inmates subscribe to jailhouse religion and leave their Bibles on their bunks when they get out, immediately returning to a life of crime. But this doesn't bother him much. For him, at least while they were seeking God, they had a chance for moral rehabilitation. What they did with it later was between them and God.

Today, Carolina is a graduate of the prison seminary and works as a missionary to other prisons. Warden Cain has sent him to four other prisons to bring the message of moral rehabilitation and spiritual transformation to others, and they are making plans to send him to a fifth.

"I talk to some of the old violent prisoners now, and I can get them to say now that they were afraid. We were afraid *not* to be violent, because if we weren't, then somebody would do violence to us." But people don't have to live this way, not in Angola—because people can change for good. Carolina knows, because it happened to him.

I wouldn't blame you if you were a bit suspicious of Carolina's conversion experience. Even if you have had your own spiritual experiences you cannot scientifically explain, you might still wonder whether his was real, or if it will last. It sounds remarkably similar to the biblical account of the Apostle Paul's conversion experience on the road to Damascus (which some have tried to explain as an epileptic seizure, sunstroke, or a psychotic episode). As a clinical psychologist, I can tell you that some things are hard to fully explain, but neuroscientists have compared the brain waves of people experiencing psychosis or epilepsy with those experiencing spiritual events like Carolina's and concluded they are entirely different neurological events. People experiencing some sort of mental disorder are left confused and terrified, while those reporting a mystical experience with God are left feeling more whole, serene, and with a new awareness of love.[1] Let me give you a bit more of Carolina's story before you decide for yourself whether or not you think his change is real.

Carolina the Missionary

Carolina's most recent missionary trip was to Rayburn Correctional Center, where he had been incarcerated years earlier. The prisoners there knew him well and were fully aware he was not above "slapping the taste out of somebody's mouth" if the occasion called for it. But the Carolina who walked in the doors on this visit was not the man they knew—he was a changed person. He had transferred his commitment to a life of nonviolence from his former girlfriend to his present relationship with God, and he fully intended to keep living this way.

"I'm no longer in prison," he explained to me. "This is my mission field. What the devil intended for evil, God is using for good."

One of the first passages in the Bible that Carolina read was the third chapter of Ezekiel. In that passage, God sends Ezekiel to minister to his own people, who speak his language, rather than to a foreign people who didn't. This gave Carolina a clear direction for his life. His mission was to take the message of God's transforming love to every prisoner he knew, especially to the most violent ones. These were his people. These were the ones whose language he could speak.

"This is one of the things I say to people who are setting up programs in prisons: do not overlook the most violent inmate in your prison," he told me. "Reach out to him; chances are nobody has ever given him a chance."

The first thing Carolina did when he got back to Rayburn was, indeed, to walk up to the most violent inmate in the prison and begin to talk to him about God. As I described earlier, Carolina has an unmistakable intensity about him. You feel his presence, even when he is not speaking, and it is impossible to ignore him when he is. As you can imagine, disagreeing with Carolina might feel uncomfortable. I should mention that, by the end of our hour-long conversation, I felt totally safe being completely alone with him. Rather than fearing Carolina might do me harm, I had the sense there wasn't anyone in the world who could hurt me as long as I was sitting with him. But then, we weren't in any disagreement.

Apparently, this first man he spoke with at Rayburn wasn't getting his way in the conversation, so he decided to solve their difference of opinion by punching Carolina in the mouth. A very primitive, but effective, way of getting someone to shut up. What was Carolina's response? "I didn't hit him or hurt him. I just held him down on the floor until security came. Then I got up and embraced him."

This type of event does not go over well in prison environments. Carolina had embarrassed the man by holding him down, and this particular inmate had an equally violent friend who took it upon himself to defend his reputation. In prison terms, Carolina did not *get his issue*, and it was up to this man to seek revenge. He caught Carolina sitting on a bench and hit him four or five times before Carolina even knew what was happening. Carolina stood up, fully intending to fight the man.

"That was my full intent. To entertain this fool," he told me. Decades of conditioning sprang into action within seconds. But as he stood up and looked at the man, a peace came over Carolina, one that he had never experienced in a situation like this before.

"The only way I can describe it is to say that I felt, 'Father forgive them for they know not what they do.' So I took a step into the dude, and I told him, 'Buddy, it's okay. I forgive you.'"

In response, the man beat Carolina all the way down to the floor. Security had to pull him off. Spitting blood, nose bleeding and face swollen, Carolina struggled to his feet, stepped into the man, and hugged him again. As the guards carried the man away, Carolina told him that he forgave him, and that he loved him.

Fortunately, the entire event was recorded by security cameras, so Carolina was not sent to solitary confinement for fighting. The prison authorities were not sure how to deal with the situation, so when his attacker came out of solitary confinement, they placed him in Carolina's dorm—as if to imply that Carolina was too powerless to ever confront the man again.

"Boy, did that hurt," was Carolina's response.

This is something that is unheard of in prisons. After a fight like that, inmates are generally separated for their own protection. In a dramatic act of defiance, the man went right to his bed to lie down and go to sleep. For this man to think that Carolina was so afraid of him that he could just go to sleep right in front of him was the ultimate form of humiliation for Carolina. Previously, this act of disrespect would certainly have cost the man his life.

"You know that I'm fixing to kill him, don't you?" Carolina whispered to God.

"No, you are not. You are going to love him," was God's reply.

"No, I'm going to kill him, and then *you* can love him," Carolina bargained back.

"No, you are not." God's response was clear.

Carolina was torn between forty years of training to never lose a fight and a new experience of love he couldn't get around. While Carolina was wrestling with God, the man woke up and asked someone for a cup of coffee. Hearing again the voice of God telling Carolina to love him, he took a bag of coffee out of his own box and put it on the man's bed. He saw the man look around, unable to tell who did it. He then asked someone for something to eat, and when he wasn't looking, Carolina put some food on his bed. This went on for a couple of weeks until someone finally told the man who was doing it. Indignant and somewhat confused, the man approached Carolina.

"Hey, you been puttin' that food on my bed?" he asked.

"Yup, and I'm getting sick and tired of it," snapped Carolina.

"What?"

"That's right. I'm fed up with giving you what I want you to have. This time, you are going to make out a store list, and I'm going to go and get you what *you* want, not what *I* want you to have."

The man stared back at Carolina with a strange look on his face and then did exactly that. He filled out a store list for $25 (an exorbitant amount in prison economics) and kept doing the same for the next three months.

"You are just not going to quit, are you?" Carolina pleaded with God.

"You are going to love him," was all he heard back.

In the prison environment, when someone beats you up and you are forced to go to the store for him, you are paying *draft*. This puts you in the weaker position and sets you up for continued abuse. Typically, the dominant inmate does whatever he wants to the weaker one, up to and including forced sex acts. In prison life, when you are beaten into submission, that submission is total—at least, that's normally how it goes. But this was different. Carolina wasn't submitting to the man; he was surrendering to God. And somehow, the other inmate knew it. Carolina was not giving this man these things out of fear but was motivated by some force the other prisoner had never experienced before. Something inescapably powerful was happening to him. It's just that the inmate had no way of understanding what it was.

Finally, after three months of this, the man came to Carolina and sat on his bed. The two inmates sat there staring at each other with an intensity you could never fully know unless you meet someone like Carolina someday. And then it happened. The prisoner who had beaten Carolina down to the ground, the same one who had been demanding draft from his defeated prey for the past three months, looked Carolina square in the face and starting crying. This is just not something that you ever see in prison. Well, unless you are Carolina.

"I can't do this anymore," the man said. "I can't eat anything else that you give me. I'm sorry; please don't give me anything else."

"I'm not giving you anything," Carolina said. "God is. This is all from God. He doesn't want you to live a life of destitution and despair. My God tells me that if I see a man in need, then I am obliged to care for that man."

In that moment, a very violent man who had known only how to dominate and humiliate others was overwhelmed by a power he could not put into words—and he was changed. Carolina started meeting with him regularly, studying the Bible with him and encouraging him to follow God. Eventually he, too, was *born again*. Carolina had engaged in a power struggle with one of the most violent inmates anywhere, and even though he never laid a finger on the man, he ended up overpowering him—with love. When it came time for Carolina to leave Rayburn and return to Angola, the inmate cried, embraced Carolina, and said, "I don't know how I'm going to make it without you. Who is going to tell us about God?"

"God will," Carolina replied.

Carolina received a letter from another man at Rayburn recently, letting him know the man who beat him is still telling everyone about him. He tells them that Carolina "reduced me to love."

"Amazing!" I said as Carolina finished this story.

"No—miraculous!" was Carolina's reply.

I think he is right. At the close of my conversation with Carolina, the warden returned to collect me. He and Carolina exchanged a few more words regarding Carolina's potential missionary trip to a neighboring prison. No doubt the event I just described was on the warden's mind, and he was questioning whether or not this was really the best way to spread his program of moral rehabilitation. Like me, he has to also consider whether, just perhaps, Carolina might be the *only* person who is able to get through to people like the man who beat Carolina. I certainly could not have done it.

At one point, Carolina squarely faced the warden and said, "I have only one fear in this life, and that would be to disappoint you. You know I'm ready to leave this world, but as long as I'm here, I'm going to serve God with my every breath and work as hard as I can to never disappoint you. Because I love you."

"I love you, too," replied Warden Cain.

Moral Rehabilitation

The driving principle behind Warden Cain's philosophy of corrections is moral rehabilitation. He believes this is the only kind of rehabilitation that makes any sense. Angola is the place that we send the people who have committed the worst crimes possible, so given the recidivism rate at other prisons, it is Warden Cain's belief that to rehabilitate them in any standard way might only make them better criminals if they ever did get out.

As a psychologist, I am fascinated with the process of moral rehabilitation going on at Angola. I am aware that the most serious forms of psychopathology are very difficult to treat, especially what we call personality disorders—the forms of psychopathology that display the most immoral behavior. It was only a few decades ago that we considered them untreatable, and still today it strikes fear in the hearts of all psychologists when they are referred clients with certain forms of personality disorders. If you had to give them a label, the personality disorders most psychologists would use to describe the inmates sent to Angola would be sociopath, psychopath, and antisocial personality disorder.

The *Diagnostic and Statistical Manual of Mental Disorders* (DSM) is the catalog of psychological disorders used by all psychologists. The newest edition has taken out the terms *sociopath* and *psychopath* as standalone terms and instead included them under the category of antisocial personality disorder (APD), described in this way:

Disregard for and violation of others' rights since age 15, as indicated by at least one of the following seven sub-features:

1. Failure to obey laws and norms by engaging in behavior, which results in criminal arrest, or would warrant criminal arrest

2. Lying, deception, and manipulation, for profit or self-amusement

3. Impulsive behavior

4. Irritability and aggression, manifested as frequently assaults others, or engages in fighting

5. Blatantly disregards safety of self and others

6. A pattern of irresponsibility and

7. Lack of remorse for actions

The DSM concludes its section on antisocial personality disorders with the following paragraph:

> The consensus is there is very little in the way of effective treatment for Antisocial Personality Disorder. Individuals with APD may have to be contained by the criminal justice system, through some combination of incapacitation (incarceration) or supervision and monitoring (parole, probation, or house arrest), or informal monitoring by local law enforcement to contain their harmful behaviors to others to the greatest extent possible. Incarceration may not be a deterrent to the antisocial individual, as those with APD have difficulty learning from mistakes, are rigid in decision-making, make poor decisions, and are unresponsive to punishment.

Carolina had every single one of the seven sub-features of APD when he arrived at Angola, and you only need three of them to qualify. Experts who have spent their entire professional lives studying psychopathology have concluded that there is very little in the way of effective treatment for antisocial personality disorder. And yet, here we have Carolina, a man who was likely suffering from APD for decades before his conversion experience who today is able to commit himself to a moral path and refuses to hurt another human being even in the face of life-threatening physical abuse. Whether the authors of the DSM can believe it or not, Carolina is morally rehabilitated and cured of APD.

Specialists who work in the criminal justice system have to be very specific in identifying psychological problems that underlie criminal behavior. Those specialists still use the term *sociopath* to identify a subclass of APD, and an even more disturbed classification of criminal pathology is reserved for the term *psychopath*. In general, sociopathy is a very destructive and dangerous form of APD, but it is possible for sociopaths to form attachments to others. On the other hand, psychopaths are just as dangerous, yet they are unable to form attachments and completely lack any capacity for empathy or guilt.[2] These are the most dangerous people in the world.

The experts in this area tell us that psychopaths make up less than 1 percent of the general population but about 20 percent of our American prison populations. Some believe the lack of guilt that drives this disorder may be the result of a lesion in the brain that makes a person neurologically incapable of empathy and remorse. Warden Cain uses the term *predator* to describe inmates who are incapable of change, which is the same term that the renowned expert on psychopathy Dr. Robert Hare uses to describe psychopaths who appear incapable of change.[3] Cain keeps these people separate from the general prison population because he wants to protect those inmates who are on the path to rehabilitation and change.

We don't know everything about what causes someone to become a sociopath or psychopath, but it is some combination of genetics and environmental variables. Before his powerful experience with God, Carolina would have qualified. Today, he certainly would not. Carolina experienced the miraculous combination of a spiritual transformation with a loving God and the ongoing support he needed for that transformation to last. In spiritual terms, we call this community. In psychological terms, we call it an emotional home for his pain. No matter how you describe it, the fact that there is a large community of morally rehabilitated inmates living deeply spiritual lives in the middle of the largest maximum-security prison in America is a miracle in itself. One inmate told me the only way he could describe Angola to me would be to call it the largest prison church in the world.

I think the best way to understand the moral rehabilitation in Carolina's life psychologically is to avoid focusing too much on the DSM, because it just isn't that helpful in his case. This is the problem that Zimbardo ran into when he tried to identify evil using a dispositional perspective in the Stanford Prison Experiment that I described earlier. Trying to conceptualize evil with individual personality traits doesn't help us help people like Carolina—viewing them as suffering from psychological trauma does. Viewing the inmates in Angola as having personality disorders makes us think there is very little in the way of effective treatment for them. As I discussed earlier, for some this may be true. But, I believe it is beneficial to view many of them as in need of healing from the trauma in their lives, which means they can be helped.

It is interesting to note that in the biblical account of the Apostle Paul's life-changing spiritual experience, which was so similar to Carolina's, he needed Ananias and the community in Damascus to complete his healing process (Acts 9). So, too, Carolina needed the community at Angola to come alongside of him in his. Even though the authors of the DSM may have a hard time believing it, Carolina has been healed of every single one of the seven sub-features of APD in his life. Today he follows the warden's rules, is brutally honest, refuses to engage in fistfights, has a high regard for the well-being of others, holds a position of responsibility in the prison, is remorseful for past behavior, and, most importantly, has developed the capacity for impulse control. It is not that Carolina no longer has anger or the impulse to respond with violence—I'm sure you noticed that he readily confessed those feelings to me. It's that he now has the capacity to control those impulses. He is not in denial about his feelings; he has the moral ability to regulate them. Rather than thinking of Carolina as having APD, viewing him as a man in need of a relationship with God and the healing community of Angola seems more useful.

Warden Cain believes there will always be predators who will never change, such as the psychopaths who have neurological damage that prevents them from developing the capacity for remorse and empathy. But Cain and Zimbardo believe that, given the right situation with just the right relationships, most bad behavior can change. Their belief is that the most powerful way to transform your behavior from bad to good is through the relationships with those around you, and Carolina would tell you, "especially the one you have with God." When it comes to moral behavior, in order to stay good, you have to stay connected.

Empathy

Immoral behavior results from a lack of empathy for others. For most of his life, Carolina clearly didn't have empathy. He was abusive, violent, and cruel, and he entertained himself with the suffering of others. Psychologists believe that empathy starts at birth and develops when infants mimic the behavior of others and then gradually develop the ability to play, understand, and respond to their feelings. Empathy is not just sympathy (compassion for others), but the ability to understand the other's feelings and respond to them so that they feel truly known. Typically, empathy is a natural part of the developmental process, but for some people it must be taught. In Carolina's case, that life lesson had to come in a dramatic way in order to get through to him.

From the moment God reached down and snatched the anger and hatred out of Carolina's heart, he was a changed person. A person that most psychologists would have previously diagnosed as incapable of empathy was now dedicated to the care of others because of his ability to grasp their deepest feelings in his own heart. "When you come into a man's presence, you have to ask yourself, *How do you feel?*" Carolina instructed me. This was empathy. He cared for the man who beat him in such a way that it brought the man to tears and made him feel profoundly understood. This was empathy. He recognized his warden's deepest longing for him when he said, "I have only one fear in this life, and that would be to disappoint you." This was empathy.

If immoral behavior results from the lack of empathy, then the presence of empathy is its cure. Some psychologists would describe empathy as emotional intelligence. It is self-awareness, the ability to regulate your emotions, the ability to grasp the emotions of others and the social skill to interact effectively.[4] If you have those capacities, then you will be able to be a moral person. If you don't, then you probably won't.

Warden Cain's belief that a moral person is the opposite of a selfish one makes sense. The criminologists who study psychopaths boil the pathology down to selfishness. Psychopaths lack empathy and only care about themselves. What they want is all that matters to them; the needs and feelings of others don't. While psychopaths are an extreme example of a lack of empathy, I think we can all learn from their mistakes. A lack of empathy makes you selfish, and the capacity for empathy improves your moral character.

Most of us gain the capacity for empathy through normal development. Some people, such as Carolina, missed out. But we all need to recognize the importance of empathy in our lives and to constantly work at being more empathetic. If being a person of good character is your goal, it is important to recognize that you need trust and vulnerability in order to develop empathy.

Carolina's first experience of trust and vulnerability was when he finally met someone he wouldn't hurt. He was willing to surrender a lifelong commitment to self-preservation and make himself vulnerable to another human being. There was no obvious benefit to him for doing this, but he was a changed person for having done it. This prepared Carolina for the ultimate act of trust and vulnerability, which was to believe in a God that loved him when he had no physical evidence in his life to lead him to this conclusion. Today, Carolina is self-aware, regulates his emotions, grasps the emotions of others, and has the social skill to interact effectively (well, most of the time). In short, Carolina has developed the capacity for empathy, and empathy cures selfishness.

If you are interested in doing some growing in the area of character in your own life, then perhaps there are some lessons here for you. Instead of vague New Year's resolutions to try to be a better person, or restrictive diets to punish yourself into better physical shape, perhaps you should consider working on empathy by starting with trust and vulnerability.

An Emotional Home for Pain

Carolina described his family as dysfunctional. We could add alcoholic, abusive, chaotic, and a number of other terms to that description, but one thing is for sure: his family life offered no helpful tools for dealing with his pain. Pain was to be endured in order to be a *conqueror.* Like in most abusive families, the ironic tragedy was that the people that were causing Carolina the most pain were the very ones he needed to turn to for help, and that made it completely impossible for him to make sense of his suffering. This resulted in decades of acting out and destructive behavior, all rooted in his unhealed pain.

A common misdiagnosis that psychologists make is to mistake people suffering from trauma as those having personality disorders. When he first came to Angola, almost any psychologist would have diagnosed Carolina with a severe personality disorder. But while relationships damage us, they also heal us. We know that childhood trauma damages the areas of the brain that govern impulse control, but we also know that a regulating community of healthy relationships heals that damage and fosters the development of the areas in the brain that have to do with tolerance and good decision making.

Psychologists have found we can endure almost anything if we do not have to endure it alone.[5] This is the difference between psychological injury and psychological trauma. Psychological injury results from emotional damage we suffer from overwhelmingly painful events in our lives, but psychological trauma results from suffering that same damage when we have to suffer it alone. Everyone needs help to process pain, make sense out of it, and develop the courage to endure it honestly. Until he came to Angola, Carolina never had that.

The two greatest miracles in Carolina's life were his conversion and his community. In the community of deeply spiritual inmates surrounding him, Carolina finally found for the first time in his life an emotional home for his pain. Never before had he felt understood, and only when he felt understood could he begin to feel safe enough to admit to a wealth of feelings that he didn't even know he had. Because he can now confess his pain, guilt, grief, and fear, this opens him up to experiences of joy, love, and meaning that he never knew existed. It doesn't help to think of Carolina as having a personality disorder for which there is no effective treatment, but it does help to view him as a trauma survivor who has finally found a home for his pain.

Carolina is a dramatic example of the need for an emotional home for pain, but everyone has this same need. Think about your own life. If the people who have hurt you in life are the very ones you have needed to turn to for comfort, then it may not have been a safe place for you to call home. Perhaps you need a safe community now.

No community is perfect, and even religious communities can be dysfunctional. Because communities are composed of human beings, they can't help being imperfect and even hurtful at times. But at the same time, we can't stop needing each other to help us with our pain. In community, we can find an emotional home for our pain with each other. Finding that home empowers us to live more emotionally intelligent lives and achieve moral rehabilitation in whatever way we need it. If you have been disappointed in your pursuit of a safe place to call home, don't give up. If Carolina can find an emotional home for his pain in the middle of a maximum-security prison, you can find one where you live, too.

4

People Need Community to Change

"This is a community" is a common phrase you will hear at Angola. Even though it felt strange at first, I kept hearing things like "Like it or not, this is my home, and as long as I am here I am going to treat it as such." Everywhere I turned, inmates were referring to this maximum-security prison as a family or their society. Their awareness of their community identity and sense of responsibility for it was striking. These prisoners, almost all of whom had lacked social consciousness before coming to prison, have somehow created an environment with a social awareness that was powerful enough to make a very real difference in each other's lives. The general population at Angola has been transformed from a collection of self-centered individuals into an influential community of change.

Psychologically, this is important. Psychologists used to think individuality was central to psychological health. Personal power, individual intelligence, ambition, and self-confidence were the goals of psychotherapy just a few years ago. Developmental researchers called this *separation and individuation*; it was based upon studies of infant behavior, and they believed that independent thinking was the hallmark of the mature individual. This has all changed.

Psychological researchers are now talking about mutuality, social intelligence, interdependence, and self-other relationships as the basis of mental health. Separation and individuation are no longer the goal of psychological treatment, and the social scientists who study infant behavior are seriously questioning the scientific methodology of that earlier research. They now conclude that someone can only be a healthy person if they maintain healthy relationships with others throughout our lives. Leading psychoanalysts are now calling independent thinking *the myth of the isolated mind*.[1] By this they mean that our ways of thinking are actually influenced by the thoughts of others both past and present, so thinking you can make up your own mind is really more of an illusion than any of us would like to admit. You have an individual brain, but what we refer to as the mind is actually a property of relational interactions. Being an isolated individual is no longer a sign of health, and lone rangers are no longer our heroes.

Think about it. The people who consider themselves real individuals first have to look around and see what everyone else is doing in order to choose to stand out from the crowd. They say they are independent thinkers and that they march to the sound of a different drummer, but the only way they know that is to consider what everyone else is thinking. In other words, individuality is a relational construct. We can't get away from it—we are fundamentally relational beings.

Leading psychologists now say we are relational creatures seeking meaning from our emotional and spiritual experiences with each other. Our individual identities are the result of millions of relational events that, over time, combine to give us a sense of who we are. You are not only who you were born to be but also who you were shaped to become through all the relationships you have had. Of course, your personal biology is uniquely yours, but that biological makeup can only be expressed within the context of other relationships. You are who you are because of the community that raised you, and you can only be the best version of yourself if you remain connected to a community now.

This is one of the central problems for every prisoner who ends up at Angola. So many of them became disconnected from their families or communities and tried to go their own way. Some of them hooked up with gangs or other disenfranchised people to try to recreate a sense of community, but these detached individuals only reinforced their lack of connection with the larger community and their anger at feeling so alone. This disconnection results in painful feelings of being misunderstood, insignificance, and shame for simply being who you are; which only leads to making people feel defective and incomplete. That is the inevitable result of being disconnected from the community of others.

Most of the inmates at Angola experienced violence and abuse in their lives prior to incarceration. But, as we have discussed, what made all those psychological injuries traumatic was that they were forced to suffer alone. We were not created to do well alone, and there are no better examples of this than the tragic lives of the inmates at Angola.

It is no wonder each of these individuals lost their moral

compass. They were trying to do the impossible. Being severed from meaningful relationships, they had to make up their own rules to survive. If you are disconnected from the community that shapes your identity, you are left to try to shape one on your own. Fear and panic sets in, and you start to make choices out of desperation. The need for physical survival takes over. Any thought of right or wrong in terms of what you do to others is eclipsed. Civilization is not possible when self-preservation at all costs is your dominant motivation. Because then, the only thing you know to be true is that you have to survive.

Spiritual truth is not the kind of truth you can understand intellectually; you can only come to know it through a personal encounter. Ironically, the founder of the largest religion on the planet never tried to establish a religion. Jesus sacrificed his life, pointing us all to better relationships with God and each other, rather than religious doctrine. He taught that encountering this type of truth defines us as human beings more than any other truth or knowledge we could ever achieve.[2] He sacrificed his life in service of relationships—the relationship he had with the God who sent him and the relationships he had with the people he came to love. A deepening of our spiritual relationship with God only leads to a deepening of our relationships in community with others.

This is why the sense of community at Angola is so powerful. The inmates seeking this kind of spiritual truth discover their need for meaningful relationships with each other. Their identity depends upon it—if we can only know who we truly are in relationship, then our very lives depend upon the quality of the community around us. Instead of feeling insignificant, as they did in the past, the inmates of Angola discovered that they matter, and at the same time they discovered that every other person around them matters as well. You see, just as self-hatred and the abuse of others are inextricably bound to each other, so too are self-love and the love of others interdependent. You can't truly love yourself without loving others, and as you love others, you can't help feeling more lovable yourself.

The science of psychology confirms this spiritual truth. Our relationships not only matter but define us. Without healthy connections we disintegrate into the selfishness and immoral behavior that is the basis for all our social ills.

In his decades of psychological research on understanding evil, Zimbardo concluded that dehumanization is at its core. The "guards" in his original study were instructed to create fear and boredom in the "prisoners," and they forced those prisoners to do meaningless tasks as they swore at them in demeaning ways in their hospital-gown uniforms, using only numbers to identify them instead of their names. The less the guards viewed themselves as having a real relationship with their prisoners, the more abusive their treatment of them became.

Christina Maslach, who had the moral fiber to call for an end to the Stanford Prison Experiment, went on to marry Zimbardo and became an internationally respected psychologist herself. She has spent the past four decades developing a reputation as an expert on the psychology of individuation. Perhaps she was trying to understand what it would take for someone to stand up to evil like what was happening in the Stanford Prison Experiment, and to have the courage to speak up and do the right thing when necessary. After many years of research, she no longer thinks of individuation as differentness; instead, she now conceptualizes it in terms of *high social impact*. What gives us the most powerful sense of identity is not our individuality or the courage to act on our own but our ability to influence and connect to others. Just as spiritual teachers have taught for thousands of years, psychologists are coming to understand that we are fundamentally relational creatures. The timeless and crucially important principle here is that people need community in order to change for good.

Chief

"Come over here—I want you to meet somebody," Warden Cain called to me across a crowded room of inmates. We had both attended a worship service in the heart of the prison and I was just returning from a restroom at the back of the building that I had spied earlier. I have to admit I was a bit uncomfortable going into the restroom alone, but there was a sign on the door stating *No Offenders Allowed!!!* Despite the disturbing choice of language on the sign, I was hoping it meant I would be safe using this particular bathroom. Why I thought six thousand murderers, rapists, and armed robbers would respect such signage I don't really know. But, fortunately my trip to the restroom was uneventful.

"Dr. Baker, this is Chief," the warden said. "And Chief, I want you to meet Dr. Baker. He's here doing some research."

Chief's real name was Wilfred, and the Department of Corrections knew him by yet another name, so knowing how to address him was confusing at first. I was reticent to use the name Chief to refer to a Native American man—I worried it would be offensive. But as I was to learn, not only did he want to be called Chief, but it was very important to him to be known that way.

Chief was born in Canada to Native American parents.

His family lived in a Native American community, didn't speak English, and were very poor. His father worked odd jobs as a carpenter and his mother took care of their seven children full time. Chief knew they were poor, and he knew that white people didn't think much of them. He can still recall being chased off beaches and discriminated against for being Native American. It was obvious that those memories still sting to this day.

"We were poor, very poor. Which is how I ended up in the States," Chief said.

"What do you mean?" I asked.

"They called it *the scoop*," Chief went on. "It was a process of assimilation into the white culture. It happened to thousands of American Indians in the '60s and '70s all over the United States and Canada. The same thing happened in Australia."

"What happened?" I asked.

"Well, they created a law in Canada. If you were an Indian and you couldn't provide enough financially for your children, then they only allowed you to have two. But my parents had seven. Which meant the social workers ended up taking five of my parents' children away."

"That's terrible. How could they do that?" I asked.

"My mother couldn't understand English. So when the social workers came by, she thought they were coming to offer us government assistance of some kind. They went back and forth, and my mom thought we were signing up for financial aid or some kind of help, so she signed all their documents thinking that is what was happening. But when she took me and my sister down to the government office, they put some pictures in front of me and told me they were my parents. But I said, 'No, those are not my parents.' Then I looked up, and two men in uniform were escorting my mother out of the building. That is the last time I ever saw my mother."

"Oh my gosh," I gasped.

"The next thing I know, I was on a plane to here. My mom signed me away, and she didn't even know it. She thought she was signing up for some kind of subsidies, but she was signing away the rights to her children because the government thought they were too poor to take care of them. They said it was child abuse. Did you know in my native language, we don't have a word for *orphan*? The village raises the child where I come from. The thought that someone could take away your children had never even occurred to my parents. That's just not what we do."

In a bizarre adoption process, Chief was brought to New Orleans to be raised by a middle-class family under circumstances that were so confusing to him that he didn't even know how to talk about it. He remembers praying to God after his adoptive parents took him to church for the first time, pleading, "Jesus, I'm sorry. I wasn't bad. Please let me go home."

But this was a petition that would go unanswered no matter how many times he prayed. The social workers convinced him that his parents wanted to send him away and that he would be much better off with the standard of living that his new parents could provide him. Chief didn't think so, but he was too young to know what to do, so he was forced to resign himself to his new life. Unfortunately, he never felt that he really belonged.

His new family tried their best to make a home for Chief. They sent him to private schools, gave him his own room, put him in the Boy Scouts, took him to church—all to assimilate him into their culture. But it never worked.

Chief was disconnected from his people, and, try as his adoptive parents might, he was never going to be white.

Not surprisingly, Chief started skipping school, drinking, and getting into trouble. His first overdose from alcohol abuse was at the age of thirteen, and his parents tried to hospitalize him in a chemical dependency program. It didn't take. When he got out, he just drank even more. After he was arrested for stealing a car, his adoptive father pleaded with him to change his ways and even got down on his knees to ask Chief, "What am I doing wrong?"

"You should have thought about that before you took me away from my world," was all Chief could say.

So his parents just gave up. His adoptive mother fell into a depression, and his new father turned to alcohol to solve his problems. Things were not going well at all. Chief barely made it through high school, and he moved out as soon as he could. He didn't know any other Native Americans, and nowhere felt like home.

Instead of assimilating into the white culture, Chief tried to assimilate into the black one. Unfortunately, the community he found was an angry and violent one. By the age of twenty, he had been involved in numerous crimes and ended up fathering a son. Eventually Chief was arrested for driving the getaway car in an armed robbery that resulted in a man being shot and almost losing his life. He was convicted as a principal in an attempted murder case, and in Louisiana that's the same as having committed the crime yourself. He was sentenced to prison for 149 years.

At first Chief was sent to the Orleans Parish Prison, which was a terribly violent place. Not being a very violent person himself, Chief turned to religion to protect himself. He now refers to this period in his life as his "stint with jailhouse religion," or an attempt to be a spiritual guy who talked about God and religion not because he sincerely believed in it but because he wanted to distinguish himself from the culture of violence that surrounded him. He would quote the Bible to the other inmates, read their mail to them if they couldn't read, and try to be as helpful as he could. He knew he wasn't a predator, so he tried desperately not to become someone's prey. All around him he saw predators raping other prisoners, daily fights, and inmates stabbing other inmates for half a sandwich. It was incredibly frightening, especially for someone who never fit in anywhere his whole life.

Fortunately for Chief, he was transferred to Angola two years later. There was a different air about this prison that he could feel immediately. In 1996, there was still violence and sexual abuse to contend with at Angola, but things were changing, and Chief could feel it. In his words, "You either had to be a good boy or a bad one. But if you wanted to be a bad boy, then you had to respect the game. You couldn't mix the two."

He found positive programs to get involved with and eventually enrolled in the seminary to educate himself. He thought if he could present the image of a college boy, then perhaps he could find a way to stay alive. In his mind, it was the safest way to go. He sought out the older inmates and tried to carve out an identity for himself motivated by pure self-preservation. Chief wrote in his diary at the time that every day was like learning how to swim over and over again. He felt like he was drowning, desperately gasping for air while trying to stay afloat.

Then Chief finally came across one of the programs to foster moral rehabilitation at Angola that became a powerful source of change in his life. Because he had developed friendships with some of the older inmates, many of his friends were starting to have physical problems simply because they were growing old. When a couple of his inmate friends died of age-related illnesses and he couldn't go and visit them, Chief was very disturbed. He wasn't an uncaring criminal, so Chief set out to join a new program the warden had set up at Angola, one that would allow him to help his friends and care for them when they were facing death from natural causes.

Most of the prisoners sent to Angola are expected to die there. Despite the fact many of them will grow so old that their age alone will render them incapacitated, the people who sent them to prison want them to spend every day of their remaining lives there. The result is that Angola is rapidly becoming one of the largest old-folks homes in America. And it is extremely expensive to medically care for dozens of elderly inmates in a maximum-security prison.

To address this problem Warden Cain established a prisoner-run hospice program. Select volunteer inmates are trained to provide desperately needed hospice care to dying inmates who have no one there for them. They bathe them, feed them, clean up after them, and provide assistance to inmates dying from cancer, Alzheimer's, thrombosis, or some other terminal condition. As you can imagine, very few of the prisoners want any extreme measures taken to prolong their lives at Angola, but they all desire a humane exit from this life with as much dignity as possible in whatever time they have left.

So Chief applied to the hospice program—but he didn't get in. It takes a special person to do this kind of work. He tried to keep a clean prison record and demonstrate that he was the kind of person who could care for others during their dying days, but the admission process was very selective.

Sometimes in life, however, opportunity presents itself when you are least looking for it. Although Chief had not been admitted to the hospice program, he had worked hard to earn a place in the prison rodeo, which meant he had the opportunity to be around a number of freepeople during the rodeo events. This was a privilege and an immense responsibility. If an inmate didn't conduct himself properly during a rodeo, he would lose significant freedoms for a long time as a consequence for his misbehavior. It was very important to the warden for the inmates at the rodeo to display to the public that they were changed people.

At one particular rodeo, one of the women running the events had brought her son with her. This was not unusual, as many people brought their adolescent children with them to expose them to the life lessons that can be learned at Angola, especially the lesson that you will shape your path in life based upon the decisions you make. Every inmate at Angola will tell you that even one wrong decision can change your life forever. During this rodeo, the woman's son was asking the inmates for cigarettes because he was too young to get them easily for himself. While some of the inmates were willing to do this, Chief was not. The way Chief put it to me was this: "I don't need anyone looking over my shoulder to see if I am morally rehabilitated. I choose the right thing. That's just who I am now."

The boy became angry with Chief and told his mother unflattering things about him, thinking he would get Chief in trouble. The opposite happened. Her response was to recommend him for the hospice program. In her view, if Chief would do the right thing when no one was looking, then this is just the kind of person the prison would want caring for its aging helpless inmates who had no one looking out for them.

This was the beginning of a life-changing process for Chief. Until he cared for his first patient in the program, he had never laid his hands on another human being in a loving way. He had been broken before, but he told me that this experience "broke him all the way." He came face to face with death over and over again for the next several years, and being in the presence of a human life passing from this world to the next that many times changes you.

One of the first inmates Chief was assigned to was a well-known criminal whom he had read about before meeting him. The inmate refused to talk to Chief at first. He was a hard man, but one who had been made helpless because of his condition. Chief bathed him, broke his food up with his bare hands so he could eat it, changed his diapers, and even changed his catheter when he needed it.

"You have to understand, I'm not Catholic, I'm more of a Hebrew," Chief explained. "I don't pray with you, I don't touch you, we don't do that."

Even though Chief graduated from the Christian seminary in the prison, he referred to himself as a Hebrew. I gradually came to understand that over the course of the past several years, Chief had redefined himself as a spiritual man who was more interested in the Jewish theology of the Old Testament than in Christian theology. I think this was a part of Chief's ongoing pilgrimage to find his cultural identity in the midst of the larger black-and-white world in which he lived. He never felt like he belonged anywhere after he left Canada, so it was no surprise that he saw himself as different from everyone else in Angola. It took me a few minutes, but the more he talked the more I saw it as a compliment to the community at Angola for Chief to be allowed to assert his difference. No one criticized him or judged him for it. He had gone through all the same Bible courses that every other seminary graduate had taken. He had heard all the same lectures and sermons. And Chief had come out of this experience defining himself as "more of a Hebrew." No one disapproved of him or excluded him from their community because he saw himself as different. Instead, they welcomed him as a fellow rehabilitated moral person trying to find his way.

"I wake up every single day and choose to do the right thing," says Chief. "The system doesn't care about me; they've shown me that. I would be free by now if I had been arrested in Canada, but because of the laws here, I will probably never get out. No one cares. So I am going to live out the rest of my life in the way I want to, and to me that means doing the right thing so when I go to bed each night I can lay my head down feeling good about myself. That's the only type of religion that matters to me. Not some pie-in-the-sky focus on heaven when I'm gone; what matters to me is how I treat my neighbor now. I want to be the kind of person you would want as your neighbor. That's what matters to me."

So this is the kind of person Chief has become. He could tell story after story of the inmates he helped pass from this life into the next. One inmate lost his motor skills and his ability to talk, but he could still think as clearly as you or I can. Chief had to develop a whole new language of head movements, slapping hands together, and anything else they could think of to communicate. And when the time came, Chief was there for the last minutes of the man's life, waiting for that last heartbeat that would pronounce his death.

"I saw it," Chief said. "His spirit, which in Hebrew can also be called his *spark*. That last glimpse of life that finally leaves the body and moves on. It was profound, and an honor to be the one person to see that person take his last breath on earth. I just can't explain it, but it changes you. Whatever measure of humanity I may have lost that caused me to be sent to prison I gained back right here in hospice."

The inmates consider hospice to be more like a freeworld atmosphere than a prison. There's no posturing for position, no threat of violence or oppression, and the obvious awareness that the prisoners in hospice are "getting out" soon. Constantly dealing with life and death is a sacred space for Chief. Working in hospice has proven that he is a changed person and that the change in his life is sincere. This wasn't like the jailhouse religion he had used in the past to protect himself from predators. This was coming from a genuine compassion somewhere deep inside Chief that he never knew he had.

At first, some of the other inmates made fun of Chief for changing diapers and bathing people after they soiled themselves. But it didn't matter to him. Chief had found his connection to humanity, the one that had been taken from him as a child. Caring for those who could not care for themselves changed Chief because as he learned to love others, he began to feel God's love for him. He had never thought of himself as a bad person; he was just someone who had lost his way. He didn't feel cared for until he cared for someone else. And he is a changed person because of it.

"There was this one guy about to cross over," Chief told me. "He had been locked up for longer than I have been alive. I had bathed this person and cared for him, done everything I could for him but I still had this nagging question, 'Is he ready?' I mean I was compelled to put my hand on his arm at that moment. I told you I don't do that, but in this instance I felt I had to. You see, I also work part-time as an advocate for the inmates at disciplinary hearings. I have studied the law so I represent them when they need it. So in this case I had this strong urge to stand in this person's stead. I felt the urge to pray for him, but I didn't know what to pray, so I asked God in the name of *Yeshua* to please hold him in his hands. That moment really affected me. I don't really tell many people things this private, but I guess it's experiences like that which confirm to me the reality of the change in my life."

When it came time to consider this person's passing from this life to the next, it was the Hebrew term for Joshua or Jesus that came to his mind. Chief always felt he was different, neither black nor white. So calling himself Hebrew just seemed to fit. He never felt like he truly fit in anywhere, but I think in Angola he found the best fit that he has had yet. He feels welcomed and loved, even if he needs to call himself Chief or a Hebrew to maintain the sense that he has a different identity from the larger culture around him. He is still hurt over how he was forced to assimilate into a different culture from the one in which he was raised, and the inmates of Angola love him too much to traumatize him again by forcing him to assimilate completely into theirs. They don't seem care what he calls himself, they care about the quality of the life he lives.

"Social scientists would say that if you took all of the elements of my life and put them together you would get a different person than the one I turned out to be," Chief explained. "I didn't turn out to be the person that the textbooks said I should have."

I was starting to think the same thing about many of the inmates I met at Angola, so I was interested in where Chief was going with this.

"My circumstances were compelling me in a particular direction," he went on, "but I didn't turn out that way. You see, I believe there is a purpose to my life. My Native American people are on the brink of extinction, and I want to help. Wasting away here in the South is not what I was born to do."

"Your life seems to have been one big identity crisis that got you where you are today," I said. "Life seems to be asking you, 'What type of person are you going to be?'"

"I choose compassionate," Chief replied. "I have stood up and said, 'I don't choose hate and callousness. I have had to walk away from all of that. I have been shot, stabbed, beaten down, and I have tried to kill myself several times. I've been homeless, eaten out of garbage cans, and the mother of my son killed herself when I was sent to prison. My life has been hell, but I choose compassion."

Uncharacteristically, I was pretty much speechless at this point.

"In the twenty-eight years that I have been incarcerated, prison life has been horrible, but prison itself has not been the most difficult thing for me to overcome. It's being away from my family, and the way I was taken from them. That's been the thing that has haunted me. My natural connection to my family was taken away from me, and I was thrust into a completely different environment and expected to survive. Most of my life has been black or white. But when I look into the mirror, I see a stranger because I'm neither. I have had all kinds of identity issues and made all kinds of bad choices because of them. But now I just want to serve some compassionate purpose with my life."

"What would you like to do?"

"I've applied for an international transfer, but it hasn't come through. Maybe I can be transferred back to Canada, and I can help my people in some way. I create art, I write poetry—I mean, I would like to get involved with my people and make a difference. My life is not about prison anymore; I can see that life is more than that. I know I am here for my criminal actions, and I am sorry for the damage I caused in the lives of my victims. But I have discovered music here, and education, and I have experienced things that I believe can help my people. I could get involved in politics and make a difference."

Chief was making it clear to me that he has a moral compass now. The way he put it, "I live my life as though someone is watching me, somebody that is significant to me, whose opinion of me matters. Not that I'm paranoid or anything. But I try to pretend that someone that I care about is watching me and I want them to see the very best of me. It's this secret thing that I do that keeps me in check."

Chief has developed a conscience. A boy who was ripped from his family without any regard for his feelings, and forced to assimilate into a foreign culture that viewed him as less than everyone else, became a person who was disconnected from humanity until he landed in the Louisiana State Penitentiary. There he found himself by caring for other people. He hasn't had a conversion experience like Carolina or George, but a genuinely caring community has influenced him to be a better person. This is a community of change, and people need this kind of community in order to be the best versions of themselves.

Theologians call this *common grace*—the grace of God extends to all of humankind, so everyone benefits from it. God loves everyone, not just those who practice religion. Because two hundred inmates have graduated from the seminary in the prison, the dominant spiritual influence at Angola comes from them. So the values of love, forgiveness, humility, and caring for others have spread throughout the culture there, extending the common grace of God to all.

Chief doesn't feel forced to assimilate into the spiritual culture of Angola exactly like all the other ministers the way he felt forced to assimilate into the white culture in his childhood, and as a result, what he does feel is loved. The power of that love in the community at Angola has changed his life and empowered him to reach out with love to the lives of the people around him who are in need. Everyone has the ability to experience the love of God, no matter what language you use to describe that experience.

Christina Maslach came to a similar conclusion in her research on individuation. She originally thought that people need to stand up and be different in order to have the power to withstand the forces of evil in our world. But she conceptualizes individuation differently now. Today she thinks the greatest power to do battle against evil is expressed in the human capacity for high social impact. In other words, the highest expression of human morality is not just an individual's capacity to discern right from wrong but the ethical expression of compassion for another's pain. When we set aside our own self-interests to care for the interests of others, we are winning the war against evil in our world. The common grace of God equips us all to live this way.

Again, the important principle here is that people need community to change for good. We cannot escape our fundamentally relational nature. We can deny it, or have it abused and distorted as in Chief's case, but it is still there. Social scientists tell us that recognizing the worth in others enhances our own self-worth. Chief is a good example of this truth. We now know that treating others as valuable actually changes the prefrontal cortex of the human brain. Every hour Chief has spent caring for a dying human being is an hour of brain development that has increased his capacity to control his impulsive behavior. He is less likely to be a violent person, has greater impulse control, and is more likely to be a morally rehabilitated person because of it. This is what the community at Angola is doing: changing people. Creating a society where a person can develop a conscience and actually learn empathy. These are the very things that were missing that landed the inmates at Angola there in the first place.

Zimbardo believes dehumanization is at the core of evil. He would be delighted to know an amazing group of inmates at Angola have reversed their lives from selfish criminals to caring members of a community that recognizes the worth of others. They work alongside each other trying to better themselves, minister to each other, and even have created their own hospice program to stand by those who are passing from this life to the next. Nothing could be more humane.

"This is a community." I now know what the inmates of Angola mean when they say it.

5

Justice Means Making Things Right

Most prisons are based on a philosophy of punitive justice. The idea is simple: if you punish people for their crimes, they will learn to fear authority and stop doing them. Sadly, it doesn't work.

Angola is run under a different philosophy of justice. Having observed the system of rewards and consequences at Angola, I believe justice there means *making things right.* This concept is based on the idea that justice is not simply adjudicating right and wrong but restoring things that have gone wrong back to being right again. This form of justice is not about punishment— it is about taking action to correct injustice and restore the lives of people who have been damaged by it. From this perspective, love is more powerful than fear, and authority that inspires good behavior from within produces more lasting change than fear of punishment from someone on the outside. Coercion and control inspire fear and perpetuate violence; compassion and fairness inspire moral behavior and restore character.

In the past, evildoers were punished in the town square. This public humiliation added an additional punitive element to the judicial system's power to maintain order. But as civilizations evolved, the good people of society decided it was too barbaric to publicly flog, beat, and execute criminals out in plain view. So in the name of common decency, we invented penitentiaries. There, the wayward people of the world could be shown the error of their ways and punished until they were ready to resume their orderly role in society. This philosophy of punitive justice is still held as the morally responsible approach for the correction of criminal behavior by most prison authorities as well as much of society in general. As I explained in chapter 1, most people believe that retribution is the morally appropriate response to evil action, and the most humane place to conduct the punishment of evildoers is behind prison walls.

Most books on prison life in America come to the conclusion that our penitentiaries are based on a punitive justice philosophy. Prisons are violent, racist, and dysfunctional environments that do very little to rehabilitate the prisoners sent there.[1] Sadly, 66 percent of those released from prison are re-arrested within three years, 60 percent will still be unemployed after a year out, and those who do find jobs earn about half as much as similarly qualified people who have never been incarcerated. More than 20 percent of prisoners admitted to being raped while in prison, with some of them repeatedly assaulted as many as one hundred times a year. Most prison cultures are dominated by race-based gangs, and some prison authorities respond with violent goon-squad guards who terrorize inmates and staff alike. One study by the inspector general of the Justice

Department found illegal drugs present in nearly every one of the United States' 102 federal prisons, and in some cases it was the guards selling them to the prisoners.

Race-based gangs are a very serious business in the violent atmosphere of most prisons, as not only do they provide safety in numbers, but their leaders function as generals, controlling their troops to maintain order in what might otherwise be a brutal culture of chaos and mayhem. If a member of an Aryan gang is making too much noise and keeping people up at night, his gang leader will discipline him to prevent an attack by black or Hispanic inmates that could result in an even greater senseless loss of life than what they already have to deal with. And because most gang members on the street either end up in prison or know someone who does, the gangs inside prison serve as a kind of court system, dispensing their own version of justice on anyone who violates their code of practice even in the outside world. Sadly, the gang leaders' application of punitive justice fits with the philosophical bias of most prison systems, so the authorities allow the gang leaders' methods of control to continue. Their agenda of keeping some semblance of order takes priority over any hope of rehabilitation.

Punitive justice operates on the basis of fear and control. Behavior is controlled because people are too afraid to act otherwise. But anyone operating under this system of governance will cease misbehaving only when the threat of punishment is clearly present, not because they are morally rehabilitated. This approach to justice within prisons breeds crime, dehumanization, and recidivism. Because most prisons are run in this manner, it is no wonder Philip Zimbardo concluded that the prison experiment in America has failed.

Punitive justice might be necessary at times, but it is not the only form of justice. At Angola, a more effective alternative approach to wrongdoing is similar to what has been called restorative justice.[2] This system of justice is not about punishment, but about making things right—restoring things to the way they are supposed to be.[3]

This is the approach at Angola. Warden Cain freely admits there are consequences for bad behavior, and if you commit acts of wrongdoing you will lose freedoms as a result. But he also states openly that he doesn't ever want to take an inmate's freedom from him; it is the inmate who makes the choice to give it up. "I don't want it. He gave it back to me" is his frequent statement regarding any discipline he is required to dish out. Cain isn't interested in retribution—he wants moral rehabilitation. Just like any good parent, Cain doesn't just want his inmates to act good because they are afraid of him. He wants them to be good because they choose to be that way.

One of the most remarkable things about Angola is that almost everyone you talk to in the general population of the prison has the same unmistakable feeling toward Warden Cain—respect. The other wardens respect him, the guards respect him, and so do the prisoners I talked to. I'm sure they all know there would be consequences for misbehavior or not following through with their jobs, but it was very clear to me in my conversations with the people I talked to there that they were not motivated primarily by fear of punishment. What kept coming through to me was that the people I talked to at Angola were motivated to follow the warden's instructions out of a very profound respect for his authority. They followed his leadership not because they were afraid of what would happen if they didn't, but because it just made sense.

Punishment may be a part of justice, but an approach to justice that focuses exclusively on punishment is an incomplete one. Under punitive justice, if you are not tough on crime, the only alternative is that you are soft on it. Under the version of restorative justice I witnessed at Angola, you can actively acknowledge crime, take steps to correct criminal behavior, and work to restore the relationships damaged by it. With this perspective, you see wrongdoers as being in need of healing, forgiveness, and restored relationships. God doesn't love suffering, God loves people who suffer.

The basic problem with an exclusive focus on punitive justice is that it does not produce reform—it perpetuates violence. We all have a built-in capacity for violence and retribution. You don't have to teach children to hit back; they do that quite naturally. What you do have to teach is empathy, and people do not learn empathy by being shamed and dehumanized by punitive justice.

What I am referring to as the restorative approach to justice at Angola has the goal of making things right. This produces reform in two ways. First, the individual who has committed the transgression must be restored morally and spiritually. This requires the acknowledgment of his wrongdoing, repentance, and reconciliation with God. The individual is not just punished but reformed by a process of spiritual transformation. Second, the individual now lives in a moral way in the world. This moral rehabilitation seeks to make the whole world right, not just the individual. The individual person is restored to the way he or she should be, and then that person takes this way of being into the world with the goal of restoring it to the way it should be as well.

Making moral rehabilitation the goal of justice just makes good sense. We have two paths toward justice:

wrongdoers being punished so they suffer for their crimes but are seldom rehabilitated; and wrongdoers being restored to moral people who can then work to reform others in order to make the world a better place. It is clear to me which is the better option. From Warden Cain's perspective, this is doing corrections correctly.

Ron

Ron grew up in Appaloosa, Louisiana, just outside of Lafayette. He wasn't raised in the church, but his mother took him to the local Catholic church at Easter and Christmas because it seemed like the right thing to do. Because he didn't receive much guidance from his family, Ron grew up running with some fairly wild kids and started drinking and smoking at a young age. Fortunately, however, he didn't get into any serious trouble.

When he was fifteen, his mother became a devout Christian and began attending a small Bible church regularly. Her life had changed, and Ron could feel it. With a newfound awareness of how things should be, Ron's mother invited him to attend a revival at her new church. She was concerned about his lifestyle as well as his relationship with God, or lack thereof. It was there that Ron became a Christian for the first time. For the next year, he attended church regularly, studied the Bible, and focused on his relationship with God.

On Ron's sixteenth birthday, some of the guys from the neighborhood invited him out to celebrate. They had been his friends since childhood, so when they pressured him to drink and smoke, he gave in because he didn't want to appear as though he felt superior to them or didn't care about their friendship. At first, it was just one cigarette.

Then it was a cigarette and a beer, and then before long he was drinking and smoking just as much as he did before. It was as if nothing had changed. It wasn't that his newfound faith wasn't real; it was that the social influence of his peers on him was too great. He knew in his heart that walking away from his spiritual life wasn't right, but he allowed the influence of his friends to pull him in that direction anyway. Just like the rest of us, Ron had the power to choose his direction in life.

For the next three years, Ron was involved with the same wild kids he had been running with before, only now they were all a few years older. And as any parent knows, the bigger the kid—the bigger the problems. Everything started to escalate. Ron was drinking and smoking more and getting involved with kids who were using illegal drugs and committing petty crimes, and as the violence around him got more extreme, so did the weapons he needed to carry to deal with it. At one point, Ron got into an altercation with another kid about his age. Over the following weeks, the threats back and forth intensified to the point that Ron was scared he would get seriously hurt, or even killed, particularly because he knew this kid often carried a gun. He didn't know what to do and didn't feel he had anyone to turn to for advice, so he just reacted. When Ron found himself face to face with his rival one night, he reacted in a way that he would spend a lifetime regretting. Trying to keep from getting shot himself, Ron ran while he fired his own gun in hopes of injuring the guy. He didn't find out until later that one of his bullets had struck its target, leaving him dead.

Ron ran down the street to a pay phone and called his mother. A kid running in a criminal's world, he was in way over his head. He told his mother about what had happened and asked her to have his father come and pick him up.

When his father arrived, he took Ron back to his mother's house, where some people from the church had gathered for support. As they prayed for Ron, a tremendous sense of conviction came over him. What he had done was wrong, the way he had been living was wrong, and he knew in his heart that God wanted to make things right in his life. So, then and there, he got down on his knees and repented of everything he had done. Whatever the consequences of his actions would be, Ron knew he didn't want to keep living this way.

The next thing Ron did was to ask his father to take him to the police station because he was pretty sure they were looking for him. When he arrived, the police were somewhat shocked to see him. They didn't expect someone who was involved in a shooting to just walk into the police station and surrender. It was there that Ron learned that the man he shot was dead. And that was it—Ron's life was changed forever. Although this was his first offense of any kind, and although he was just a kid, he would now be spending the rest of his life incarcerated. When you are convicted of second-degree murder in Louisiana, you are sentenced to life without parole.

Because he was only nineteen, Ron was sent to a local jail at first. When he learned that he had received a life sentence, he cried uncontrollably. He hadn't even started living his life, and now he was going to spend the rest of it in an institution. He had turned back to God on his knees that evening with his mother and her friends, and now he needed God's help to survive the journey ahead of him. What was he going to do? How was he supposed to live now?

"When I look back over my life now, I understand the importance of mentoring," Ron told me. "I just walked away from the right way to live and got influenced by peer pressure. I didn't have any spiritually mature person who took an interest in me, so I lost my way. It's really important to me now to take an interest in other people's lives. To help them grow. I can see now how important it is to help young people deal with the temptations in life if they are ever going to mature themselves."

When Ron turned twenty, they sent him to Angola, where he was admitted to Camp A. That was in 1990, five years before Warden Cain arrived. There was a church in the prison back then, though it was not very influential or well attended. But Angola was in a time of transition. Many prisoners now in Angola arrived there in the '70s and '80s, when the prison was a notoriously violent place. By the '90s, the inmates were ready for a change. Ron felt that many inmates had grown weary of all the violence and wanted something different, but they had no idea what could make that difference.

Ron told me there weren't any race-based gangs at Angola like those in other prisons. Instead, the prisoners formed groups based upon where they were from. Inmates from New Orleans grouped together, as did inmates from Baton Rouge, or inmates who knew each other from some other part of the state. There was still a lot of violence when Ron arrived, but he was never subjected to very much of it. The entire time Ron has been at Angola, he has never been in a fight—a fact that he attributes to the grace of God.

The way he sees it is that it was perfect timing when Warden Cain came to Angola in 1995. Ron remembers the warden offering a Bible class as one of his first acts toward rehabilitation in the prison. Warden Cain sent the message right from the beginning that he wasn't there to simply punish these prisoners for what they had done. He was going to offer them an opportunity to restore themselves to a higher moral plane. Ron believes the inmates wanted an alternative experience in the prison; they just needed a warden who had a vison they could follow. When Warden Cain opened the seminary in 1996, prisoners turned out to enroll with enthusiasm. They could educate themselves, rebuild their moral lives, and restore themselves spiritually. Although no one used the term *restorative justice*, Warden Cain was practicing a form of it in the lives of people who needed it most.

"Most prisoners coming into Angola for the first time are a lot like I was—very afraid," Ron explained. "Angola had a reputation at one time, and most people still believe it is the same way now until they get here and see that it has totally changed. They think all those stories were just made up now because it is so different these days. There are still things that need to be overcome, but the church is strong here now, and everyone feels it."

This is the result of justice that we all want to see: not just individuals being rehabilitated but an entire culture being restored to the way people are supposed to live. This is the kind of justice that doesn't just punish wrongdoing, but actually makes things right.

"I think what we are experiencing here is what happens when people have hearts that have truly been broken and they are ashamed of the crimes that they have committed, so they call out to God for help, to make something out of their lives that have been broken. God is in the business of taking shattered lives and putting them back together again. That has been the experience here since Warden Cain came in 1995," Ron explained.

"Before Warden Cain, we didn't have access to Camp J, which is the worst part of the prison. They put guys there that can't function in the general population. Before, there was nothing for them, so when they were released into the general population, they would be just as bad as when they went in. But now, we have seminary graduates that are given access to Camp J, so they walk down the tiers to minister and tutor the guys there. Before, they were just in their cells doing time. Now, they've got opportunities to talk about God and get educated. Those two components are changing the lives of the most violent prisoners here so that when they get out, they have a chance to make it in the general population."

Ron explained that prison ministers preach from their own experience. They go through all the same things that every other prisoner does at Angola, and this shared experience gives them the power of authority in the lives of the inmates there. If an inmate decides to follow the advice of a prison minister, it is not because he is being coerced to do so; it is because he is being influenced by a very credible source.

Grace, or unconditional love, is a very difficult concept for most inmates. Their belief is that the things they have done have disqualified them from ever receiving love. How could anyone ever love a person who has done what they have done? The fact that God loves everyone no matter what they have done is very hard for most of them to grasp. But when they encounter grace, the impact is life-changing.

"Most of them have been told that nothing good comes out of Baton Rouge, or no one is any good who comes from New Orleans, or nothing good comes out of Angola, but when they hear that the same thing was said about Jesus, this gets their attention," Ron said. "Here is a God who understands them and can love them just the way they are, no matter what sins they have committed. That's a power-ful thing."

"We have denominations in here," Rod added, "like Pentecostal, Baptist, Methodist, Apostolic Pentecostal, Church of God in Christ, but they all really fellowship together. I have never been really a part of the church out on the streets, so I'm just going by what I hear, but we don't seem to be like how it is out there, with all the separation over doctrinal issues. In here we just preach what the Scriptures say."

That was my experience at Angola, too. I talked to inmates from several different churches, and even from different faiths, and no one seemed to care about their differences. What they all did care about was whether they were living in responsible ways. It seemed to me the inmates of Angola were very focused on putting their shattered lives back together the way they were supposed to be.

"What about the really hard-core guys?" I asked. It was hard for me to imagine how this soft-spoken Christian guy could break through to a prisoner who was still angry at the world and ready to defend himself from every threat at a moment's notice.

"Well, what we do is love on people," was Ron's characteristically easygoing reply. "We try to make contact with them to let them know we love them. We have ministers in every dormitory, so when a new inmate comes, those ministers are ready to reach out to them. We read their letters to them when they can't read well; we give them hygiene supplies and try to show them that they matter. In most cases, that eventually touches them. I have seen some of the most violent prisoners you can imagine become some of the kindest people you will ever meet. People are still afraid of them for quite some time. They have to watch them for a while before they believe they have really changed. Then they see that this is a person who will no longer hurt you—he's actually one who will help you. This is my experience of the church here in Angola."

Ron went on to articulate what I had thought when I first came to Angola.

"People probably think this is being staged," he said. "As if the warden told us to look like this or act this way. But this is everyday people living their lives every day trying to do good. They are just doing what they do every day."

"What about the inmates that you see doing bad stuff? What do you do then?" I asked.

"We hold them accountable," Ron replied. "We say, 'This is not going to happen here.' Most of the inmates here respect the pastors; it didn't used to be that way, but it is now. My life is an open book here. I can't preach one thing and then go back to my house and do something different. Over time, prisoners respect you for who you are. That builds up a rapport with even the inmates who are outside of the faith. Then they will allow me to speak to them when a crisis finally comes their way."

"Have you had to confront a man about some of his behavior?" I asked.

Ron went on to tell me of a time when he stepped in to prevent an inmate from being raped. "I let him know that I was going to be there for him in any way I could," said Ron. "And I told him if someone was putting pressure on him, then I was here to help. Because I can go to the inmate, no matter who he is, and let him know that he's got to leave my brother alone, because this person is my brother. It's our responsibility; if we see a brother going off the path, we go and get him. Like Jesus did with the ninety-nine sheep and the one that got lost."

That is powerful, I thought. In most prisons, inmates being forced to have sex against their will is just accepted. At Angola, it is not tolerated. And most surprisingly, it is not the guards or the administration who are policing the rapists—it is the prisoners themselves. This is the kind of justice that makes the most sense. Instead of focusing on preventing criminals from doing more harm, Angola focuses on transforming wrongdoers into people who can do good.

At Angola, people who previously lived troubled and immoral lives are being given an opportunity to make things right. They cannot go back into the past and reverse the wrong that they have done, but they can reverse the moral direction of their lives now. The type of restorative justice I witnessed at Angola is making things right in one of the best ways anyone could.

6

True Hope versus Wishful Thinking

The greatest enemy here is a lack of hope.

—Warden Burl Cain

Despite all the talk about God I heard from the inmates at Angola, it is not a lack of faith that presents the greatest obstacle to personal transformation in the lives of the inmates there. Perhaps the greatest barrier to lasting change is debilitating despair. To have faith that there is a God but lose hope that God will intervene for you results in very long and despairing nights. Fortunately, however, there exists a powerful antidote to despair—true hope.

Sometimes we use the word *hope* to refer to a feeling of confidence that something is going to happen in the future, like when we refer to the "hopes and dreams" that inspire us to keep working hard at whatever it is we are doing. This kind of hope inspires us because we believe good things await us in the future. But most often there is an element of doubt implied when we use the word, as in, "I hope it will happen," or "I hope we will get there on time." Now we are using hope in the sense that something may or may not happen. This adds an element of uncertainty that suggests there is something more to the word than we might realize.

Psychologists make an important distinction between two kinds of hope that can offer some clarity here. The first is called wishful thinking, or defensive hope. There is nothing wrong with having confidence that what you hope for will happen someday, but wishful thinking focuses on a positive outcome that we have decided we want no matter what the obstacles are—as if our hope has some magical power to make things happen. Magical thinking does not help us deal with the circumstances of life well. Defending against reality doesn't help; facing it well does.

Many of the inmates I talked to at Angola seemed to grasp this. These inmates don't believe in magic because they see magical power as something humans control; instead, they prefer to place the outcome of their lives in God's hands. Placing hope in an outcome that you have constructed in your own mind is risky business, since you cannot control the future with your mind. When our human desires trump reality, and the life we believe we *should* have becomes more important than the one we *do* have, we've succumbed to wishful thinking. Enthusiastically believing something is true doesn't mean that it is, no matter what religious language you cloak it in.

The main problem with wishful thinking is that it thwarts growth by preventing us from facing our pain and growing through it. Hope is a tool to deal with a difficult life, not a defensive avoidance of it. Wishful thinking might sound positive, but it isn't. Just like genuine faith, true hope embraces doubt and has the courage to face suffering rather than trying to do a defensive run around it. In short, wishful thinking is an attempt to deny the pain of your suffering, which is not something truly spiritual people do. The inmates at Angola who grasp this spiritual truth don't believe that God promises you an easy life—but God promises you a good one.

Perhaps you can remember a time when you felt uncomfortable around someone trying to reassure himself or herself with wishful thinking. It can be a bit awkward when someone is really trying to be hopeful, but you can't share in their enthusiasm because you get the feeling that their overly enthusiastic optimism is somehow masking something else. While those engaged in wishful thinking make themselves feel better temporarily, it brings with it a feeling of discomfort for those around them.

But let me offer a word of caution here. It is not always possible to discern when someone is engaged in wishful thinking. You cannot really know the inner heart of another person, so you cannot always know whether that person is acknowledging their pain and aware of the obstacles they face or just engaging in wishful thinking. Sometimes someone might be pursuing an illusory ideal out of denial, but at other times that person might be clinging to true hope out of courage. So it's best not to judge another person's hopes and dreams. Instead, try to apply what you are learning to yourself. In fact, this is probably a good principle to apply to everything you learn.

Fortunately, there is another type of hope that is different from wishful thinking, which psychologists call *restorative hope*. This form of hope involves the courage to face obstacles and realistically name each and every one of them if need be. Restorative hope has mature expectations, not magical ones. This form of hope is rooted in unavoidable reality and looks for a way out of difficult circumstances rather than believing in a fantasy that we have created in our own minds to wish them away. Restorative hope creates the possibility of growth because painful feelings are faced head on, not denied, and sees the obstacles for what they really are while seeking a pathway through them.

The famous story of Job from what Jewish scholars believe to be the oldest book in the Hebrew Bible offers an example of restorative hope. Job was a man of substantial wealth as well as a man of considerable faith in God. But then he lost his wealth, his children died, and he became terribly ill. Job had no illusions about the difficulty of his situation; but rather than clinging to a fantasy outcome for his circumstances (or blaming God, or himself) he held fast to his relationship with God: "Though he slay me, yet will I hope in him" (Job 13:15). Job found restorative hope by trusting that God would never abandon him, not clinging to a magical outcome that he might prefer. This type of commitment to searching for God in our present circumstances rather than pleading with God to change them changes the moral fiber of everyone who lives this way. True hope makes changing our character more important than changing our circumstances.

True hope that transforms us sees the significant pitfalls and, at the same time, elevates us to a better path. It helps us to realize how much power God has made available to us right now to partner with God to make a better future, rather than passively waiting for our problems go away. Wishful thinking keeps us stuck in the past because it is based upon a fictional future solution that never comes that keeps us focused on our real past problems that never magically go away. But true hope mourns the loss of past disappointments and makes room for new solutions. True hope inspires us to dig our way out of the low points in life with perseverance that transforms our character through genuine growth. It is only by honestly facing our pain that we can be changed by it. We place our hope not only in what might happen but in what is already happening now. True hope has the wisdom to learn from our present suffering rather than simply wishing it away.

Making the distinction between wishful thinking and true restorative hope is important for all of us, but it is critically important for the prisoners at Angola. The vast majority of the inmates there will die there. Their future on this earth is certain. The temptation toward wishful thinking is seductive and addictive in a maximum-security prison like this. Many prisoners in such circumstances insist they are innocent, and indeed a small percentage of them are actually found to be innocent based upon new evidence presented. This causes some to cling to ideas of pardons or overturned convictions. It is easy to see why inmates might turn to wishful thinking as a way of coping with their suffering, but true hope offers a more powerful way to face the difficult lives they lead.

Hope and Dread

There is an inextricable relationship between hope and dread.[1] You cannot have one without the other. All hope exists to combat the threat of dread, and at the heart of all dread is the possibility of hope. The more prominent our dreads become in life, the more necessary our need for hope becomes. And it is precisely at the times when our hope is strongest that our dreads are the nearest at hand.

The hopelessness of dread is toxic in a place such as Angola, so nowhere is the need for true hope greater to combat it.

Rather than making inmates fantasize about a life they are not likely to have, Warden Cain offers them the opportunity to improve the one they have now. He offers prisoners realistic rewards for good behavior and swift consequences for bad. The inmates know if someone fails, they can be forgiven and provided a chance to make up for their mistakes and be restored to the community. This gives them hope. If they accept responsibility for the life they have now inside Angola and strive to live it well, they can earn the ability to move about freely within the prison, educate themselves, create small businesses, and live a life of dignity among their peers. In fact, the degree of freedom the most responsible inmates at Angola experience is unheard of at any other prison in America. Prisoners can genuinely improve their quality of life at Angola, so the hope that you can be restored is quite real there.

Wishful thinking is an antidote to pain; it doesn't cure the underlying condition causing that pain, but it numbs us so we won't feel as bad. Even though wishful thinking may have the appearance of true hope, if we are in denial about our current circumstances, we are thwarting our ability to see how God is acting in our lives now. Make no mistake about it: none of the prisoners at Angola wants to be there, and every one of them would accept a pardon if it was offered to him. But this is not what the inmates are encouraged to hope for. Instead, they are offered the hope of improving their station in life now. Accepting the pain of their current situation and asking God for the courage to face it daily gives the inmates of Angola true hope.

Patience versus Perseverance

Patience is a virtue. It can be extremely difficult to exercise it when times are tough, because patience is the ability to wait for an outcome we can't control. There are occasions when this is precisely what you need to do. However, perseverance is not just waiting but taking action while you are doing so. True hope inspires us to be patient, but it also empowers us to persevere. Then our hope tempers our fear, as we no longer feel like victims of our suffering but soldiers in a battle in which we can make a difference. Perseverance inspired by true hope reverses the effects of learned helplessness that so many of the prisoners at Angola have suffered from their entire lives.

Perseverance is a character trait that inspires you to get up every morning, wash your face, and suit up for the day. This type of person is not only waiting on God to do good but partnering with God to find good deeds to do yourself every chance you can. And the inmates I talked to at Angola know that perseverance does not come without a price. They have learned that the only way to develop perseverance is to endure suffering with integrity. This is a character-building aspect of life that they have had to learn well.

I see this principle at work in the psychotherapy I do all the time. People come to me for help with the struggles in their lives because they hope that things can get better. What they come to understand is that whether or not their circumstances get better, *they* can get better if they focus on true hope in the midst of their pain. We call this the *forward edge* of therapy, the belief that I will be okay and that my relationships will sustain me amid my struggles. This is restorative hope, and it empowers everyone to search for the good things in his or her life today. We don't just wait for good things to happen; we look for the good things that are already happening now. Sometimes an overfocus on what we hope will happen later causes us to miss what is hopeful in what is happening now.

But this forward edge of therapy is always tied to what we call the *trailing* edge: the dread that past traumas will repeat themselves and that whatever is happening now that is good will not last. Life is difficult. No matter how wonderful your life has been, it has not been without disappointments, and like it or not you will fear being disappointed again because of what you have already experienced in the past. We call this the trailing edge because just when you think things are getting better, inevitably the pattern of disappointments that have plagued you throughout life come trailing along behind the good times. In this life, you cannot make things perfect and have them stay that way. Just like painting the Golden Gate Bridge: once it's finished, it's time to start all over again at the other end. Facing life well is a never-ending process.

These two edges of therapy are always present. When the trailing edge is in the foreground, you experience the dread that comes with how hard life is. These are the times when you fear that things will not go well and that, once again, you will be disappointed and hurt by how often bad things keep happening to you. But the forward edge is still there, waiting in the background. It is precisely when you dread the repetition of past traumas that you most need the hope that things will be okay. It is the goal of the therapist to fan the flames of this hope to give strength to all who suffer. Whether they know it or not, all people are looking for God amid their difficult circumstances. We are hardwired for the capacity to hope when things seem hopeless. We long for something good even when everything around us seems so bad. Every human being has the capacity for true hope because we were created to seek something beyond ourselves in every circumstance, especially at the times we need it most.

Perseverance means actively choosing the good amid the bad every day. Those who live this way are developing character, and this is the basis of true hope. This is not naïve optimism or denial but true optimism that is fully aware of our sufferings but chooses to look for the good that exists, no matter how hard it might be to find it.

Hope in What?

In some ways, life at Angola is very simple. Nowhere is the battle between good and evil, hope and dread, or life and death more obvious. Life has been reduced to its most basic elements there. It is no wonder that a higher percentage of our prison populations believe in God than the outside population in general. There just aren't that many distractions from the basic issues in life.

In the Old Testament, the Psalmist instructs us not to "trust in extortion or put vain hope in stolen good; though your riches increase, do not set your heart on them" (Psalms 62:10). If only they could turn the clock back, so many of the inmates at Angola would have heeded this advice knowing where the pursuit of illicit gains would get them. Hoping to get rich quick never seems more pointless than when you are serving a life sentence at a maximum-security prison. We all think we know what we want, but all too often, once we get it, we realize it wasn't what we really needed after all.

We all struggle with this. We're all tempted to place our

hope in material wealth, fame, sexual pleasure, or something else that we fantasize will provide us with happiness. So many of us live with the hope that someday our dreams will come true, and then we will have what we have been waiting for—someday.

The prisoners of Angola have been given the opportunity to seriously contemplate the point of life. What are you hoping for? Success in your career, or healing from a physical problem, or the ability to change someone else in the way you think they need to change? These are not bad things to hope for, but the inmates of Angola are forced to hope for the very most basic things of all. For a man named Hayward, once he met God at Angola, his heart turned to the most important thing he could ever hope for: a restored relationship with his son. Few things could be more basic than that.

Hayward

Hayward is currently serving a life sentence for second-degree murder. There is no hope he will ever live outside of prison walls, but despite this fact, Hayward is one of the most hopeful men I have ever met.

Hayward grew up in Slidell, Louisiana, just across the Mississippi River from New Orleans. His parents separated when he was five years old, so he grew up, like most of the prisoners in Angola, in a single-parent home. He didn't have a father figure in his life, and his mother had to work two or three jobs to support the family. The unfortunate consequence of this was that Hayward grew up without much influence from either of his parents.

"My older sister basically took care of us, so me and my siblings were on our own. That's just how it was," he told me. "So I had a very, very challenging upbringing. I was an angry young man because my father wasn't there. After a certain age, I became rebellious and made my own decisions. I moved out of my momma's house at age fifteen, and I was left to my own. Because I was just a country boy, I always worked, though. I did the same thing I saw my momma do, but I also had my past to deal with. My dad ended up in the same prison where I am now when I was still pretty young. That factored a lot in my life."

Hayward was a talented kid. He played sports and did well academically. But he had "empty spots" in his life, as he puts it, that led him in the wrong directions. He was a natural leader; people just wanted to do whatever he was doing. Unfortunately, the thing he was probably best at was fighting. In his words, "I don't know why I was blessed with that particular skill. I was just an angry young man, and I wasn't afraid of anything. But I was also just ignorant. So I grew up making my own decisions and living by my own devices."

Hayward had a very difficult time bonding with his family. He was close to his siblings, but he was furious with his father and angry with his mother along with all her relatives. So he quit high school even though he was doing well. He was offered a promotion at his job, so he took it. It provided him with more money to hang out in clubs and bars and to buy drugs. All of this inevitably led to Hayward to getting into more fights, which cultivated a group of relationships that grew increasingly more violent and antisocial.

At one point, Hayward's girlfriend became pregnant with his child. This was a surprisingly sobering event in his life, given his lack of regard for most people. Moved by the impact of having a son, he decided that he wanted to be a father, but he had no idea how to do it. His relationship skills were so poor that he ended up driving his girlfriend away before their child was born. Even though he wasn't with her anymore, when his son, Tyler, came into the world, Hayward felt a pull in his heart to be a dad. "That was my heartbeat," he told me. But he had been so abusive to Tyler's mother that she completely cut off her relationship with Hayward and refused to ever let him see his son—which only made him angrier.

Feeling lost, Hayward got a job that was good enough to support his nightlife habits and a series of unstable relationships. He had a close relationship with his sister, but when she died of cancer, he went off the deep end, quit his job, and threw himself into a life of binge drinking. To make things even worse, he then learned his live-in girlfriend was cheating on him, and she moved out. Now jobless, a friend was able to convince him to join him in a home burglary, assuring Hayward that no one would be home. Tragically, the owner was home and suffered a heart attack and died during the burglary. Frightened and alone, Hayward sought out his ex-girlfriend and desperately tried to convince her to come back home with him. When she refused, he went into a rage and stabbed her once in the chest with a steak knife he happened to have in his car—and she died.

Hayward was arrested in 1997, convicted, and sent to Parish Prison. He was just as chaotic in prison as he had been on the outside. Fighting was his thing. His reputation had preceded him, so by the time he got to prison he was well known as a violent person, and he didn't care. He thought he was invincible, that he was above it all. What he didn't realize was that underneath all that anger and violence was a world of hurt that had never been addressed, and now that he was in prison, he didn't know where to turn. He felt like his back was against the wall because he didn't have money for an attorney, and no one was interested in helping him, much less listening to anything he had to say. So Hayward shut everyone out; no one wanted to listen to him, so he didn't care about anyone else either.

Then, Ramsey entered the picture. Ramsey was with a prison ministry that went to prisons on a regular basis, just to talk. Because Ramsey was from Slidell, he wanted to talk to Hayward, and Hayward agreed to meet with him. There was something different about Ramsey. He was the kind of guy that Hayward could relate to, down-to-earth and not judgmental. It didn't seem to bother him at all that Hayward was in prison, or even why he was there in the first place. Because Ramsey was interested in Hayward, Hayward became interested in what Ramsey had to say. It was there, in Parish Prison, that Hayward first came to know God. He still looks back on it as a genuine experience, even if it didn't last.

"It was *flickerous*. It was like . . . I remember me and a friend of mine, he's up here now, was there doing a Bible study with me in a cell. It was packed because everybody knew who I was. It was like 'Wow!' Nobody could believe it. '*Hayward* is leading a Bible study?' But then I was transferred to a few other places, and then, you know, I didn't know anybody, and there's not any church going, so I kind of reverted back. It's hard to say why, it's just that I went back to my negative 'feed', what you would call normal prison culture. So when I got to Angola I was bitter, and angry. I was fighting again, and people were actually scared of me."

But Hayward had never been anywhere like Angola before. By the time he arrived, Warden Cain had already been there for four years developing a different kind of prison culture. Churches were starting up in the prison, real churches with inmate pastors and inmates with committed relationships to God. This wasn't someone from the outside telling him how he was supposed to be living his life and then getting in his car and driving home to his warm bed and loving family. At Angola, if a man talked to him about God, that man was going to be living right there with him twenty-four hours a day, and Hayward could see whether what he was talking about actually worked.

Sydney, the pastor of one of the oldest churches in Angola, had been watching Hayward since he arrived. He could see how the other inmates respected Hayward, and he had heard from some of the others about Hayward's previous spiritual conversion that didn't seem to have taken hold. So, Sydney confronted him.

"Can't you see that you've just become the product of what's going on here?" he asked. "You know man, you're a leader. You need to man up and take your responsibilities."

"Dude, you don't know me," snapped Hayward.

But Sydney didn't back down. He saw something in Hayward, and he wasn't about to let go of him. He knew every inmate there had been abandoned by the important people in their lives, and he wasn't going to be one of those for Hayward. So every chance he got, Sydney challenged Hayward to step up and be the person that God had always intended him to be.

So one day, Hayward decided to go to a church service, just "out of the blue." He had this nagging feeling that what he had experienced at the Parish Prison was real, even though he couldn't keep from sliding back to his old ways. He told me the sermon that day made him feel like someone had talked to the preacher ahead of time about him.

It was as if it was directed at him. That sermon hit him so powerfully that he got down on his knees and asked God to take control of his life. He had made a mess of it, and he was sure now that this was the best place to go to for help. From that day forward, according to Hayward, he "has never gone in reverse again."

The inmates who had come to expect Hayward to be violent didn't believe this change in him would last. But Hayward would tell them, "Look, man, I'm on a journey, so you've just got to back up. I've got to find *me*, and I'm focusin' right now."

"I could feel God's presence all over me," Hayward told me. "People didn't even know. I was just walking through them, and they were just moving out of the way. I went and got rid of all my junk. I stopped smoking. I got rid of the magazines. All that—I just threw everything away. That one night changed my life forever. I quit cursing and all that. I have only cursed twice in the last eleven years, none in the last nine. It's something that I just started taking charge of in my life. It's one of the things that I tell people all the time. I'm just an old country boy. I haven't been through the Bible college. I haven't done any extraordinary things for God. But when you are faithful to God, he will bless that. And that's where I come from. I come from a place where I know I will never be the same. I knew that he had created me for such a time as this—for greater things."

Angola wasn't like the Parish Prison. Here, inmates could be positive and focus on making themselves better people despite being in prison. Here, Hayward learned, a person could have hope. Hayward could tell the prisoners in Angola were not just naïvely optimistic or spouting religious platitudes to make themselves look good to the authorities. No, these people had real hope that was making a difference in their lives, and he wanted that, too. What Hayward didn't know was the hope that he was about to grab hold of would change his life and the lives of thousands of other people right along with him.

Hayward joined a prison church and devoted himself to following God with a sincere passion. Everyone could see the change, and after a while, no one questioned its authenticity. Then, a friend of Hayward's named Bruce, visiting from the First Baptist Church of Slidell, asked him an unassuming question that lit a fire in his belly: "What can I do for you?" The answer that jumped immediately into Hayward's mind was "Help me find my son."

The thing that had been plaguing Hayward most for years was his concern over his son. He didn't want Tyler to end up in prison like he had, and like his father had before him. Hayward was very aware that children of incarcerated people are extremely likely to end up in prison themselves one day. He had always wanted to be a father to Tyler, but he had no idea how. Tyler's mother had cut Hayward off, and he didn't blame her for that. He had been abusive and wasn't deserving of the privilege of even being around the boy.

But this didn't keep Hayward from hoping that in some way he could be a father to Tyler. Hayward started praying that God would provide a way for him to find out where his son was and open a door for him to be the father he had always wanted to be but never was. Hayward knew what his greatest hope was now—that he could be a good dad for his son.

For the next several years, Hayward tried to reach out to Tyler many times. He found out later that Tyler's mother had told him that Hayward had never wanted anything to do with him and that he was dead now anyway. Several friends of Hayward's and even his mother looked for Tyler and his mother for years, but with little success. Although they found her twice, Tyler's mother gave the wrong address and phone number so that Hayward couldn't contact her. But Hayward didn't give up. He was so intent on finding his son that he thought about him constantly. Some nights he would even wake up in a cold sweat, certain he heard Tyler's cries of "Daddy, I need you!" Answering that cry had become his hope, and now it was his passion.

Then, one day, Hayward received a subpoena in the mail, addressed to him at the Louisiana State Penitentiary. Apparently, Tyler was no longer living with his mother, and the woman acting as Tyler's caretaker had been living with a person who was abusive to her as well as to Tyler. Well, one day the man beat Tyler, only this time Tyler called the police, and they came to the house and picked him up. The state of Louisiana will not allow a child to be left in "incapable hands," so they took him out of the home and contacted his biological parents. That's how Hayward finally found out where his son was.

Hayward's passion to be a good father to his son was in full force now. He needed Tyler in his life, and now he knew that Tyler needed him in his, too. Tyler was eight years old and in desperate need of his dad. Hayward was not going to let him down, despite the fact he was serving a life sentence in a maximum-security prison. So Hayward set out on a campaign to not only intervene in Tyler's life but seek custody of him as the full-time legal guardian that he needed. Hayward set up a plan where he would ask the courts to have Tyler placed in his sister's home, where he would live, but then seek to be awarded legal custody. Then, his sister could bring Tyler up to the prison for face-to-face visitation several times a week so that Hayward could be the dad he knew he was always supposed to be. No inmate had ever been awarded full custody of a minor while serving a life sentence for murder. But that didn't stop Hayward.

It wasn't easy. Hayward had to go to court several times to argue his case. Warden Cain not only allowed him to go but sent him there free of chains, prison uniform, or anything that might make him appear to be anything other than who he was: a concerned father advocating for his son. Tyler needed his dad; and anyone who knew Hayward knew what to do about it. Each time Hayward appeared in court, he was supported by dozens of friends from Slidell who had come to believe in him. On one occasion, more than one hundred people, mostly from the First Baptist Church of Slidell, crammed into the courtroom to act as character witnesses. Over time, Hayward came to know the judge, the district attorney, and everyone in the courtroom by name. If an issue came up regarding Tyler's care, the judge refused to even hear it without Hayward being present, and he canceled court on the few occasions when Hayward couldn't make it. Hayward's desire to be a good father for his son was clear. Everyone who knew him could see it. When the day came that the judge awarded Hayward custody of his son, there wasn't a dry eye in the courtroom. This man not only wanted to be a good father for his son; he already was.

Tyler's mother was struggling with a drug addiction, and her history of relapse didn't make her appear to be the best person to care for him. The court had to make a decision: either place Tyler in the foster system or award custody to Hayward. The judge was aware of the uniqueness of the situation, and even though this had never been done before, Hayward's ability to demonstrate his heartfelt desire to be a good father to Tyler was so convincing that the judge did award him custody of his son. And now, fifteen years later, no one in the court system has regretted that decision for even a minute. Hayward had been hoping to be a good father to his son for years, and that is precisely what he became.

Tyler's mother contested the ruling, but nothing ever came of it. Each time Hayward went to court, everyone there would be waiting to greet him. In his words, "It was a God thing." The officers of the court, the child-protective agency workers, everyone had come to believe Hayward was the real thing. Here was a father fighting to help his son have a better life despite incredibly difficult circumstances. Everyone who listened to Hayward ended up believing in him and wanting to support him. On one occasion a court clerk asked Hayward, "Hey, are you from around here?"

"No," Hayward replied. "I'm just here for my son."

"Well, you're famous over here," she told him with a laugh.

An aide overhearing this jumped in, "Hayward is not just anybody. He's family up here."

As you can imagine, things were difficult with Tyler at first. He had to deal with his mother's lies about Hayward not wanting him and even being dead. When he found out the truth about his father, Tyler was angry—at his mother for lying, at the rest of his family for abandoning him, and at Hayward for ending up in prison. This wasn't the father he wanted to have, so Hayward was going to have to earn his respect. Hayward just listened at first. Tyler had a lot to get off his chest. He had been molested, abused, and neglected, and had suffered so much. But Hayward fought for their relationship harder than he had ever fought for anything before, and for a fighter like Hayward, that's saying something. They met as often as they could and wrote letters frequently. Hayward was in his son's life now, and he was committed to making a difference.

Not surprisingly, Tyler had his ups and downs over the next several years. Hayward had to ask for permission from prison authorities several times to intervene on Tyler's behalf. Tyler had to deal with other kids asking him where his dad was and claiming he must not love him if he was in prison. But, each time Tyler needed his dad, Hayward would be there for him in any way he could.

"I love you, and I'm here for you," Hayward would tell him. "Whatever is going on for you, we will figure this out together,"

Today, Tyler is in college and doing well. He only sees his dad in person about once a month because of the distance, but they talk over the phone regularly. Hayward encourages him and supports him in his own relationship with God. Tyler is involved in a local church and is becoming a man of character himself. Unlike Hayward during his own adolescence, he has a good role model to look up to for that.

You are probably wondering how Hayward became such a good father while serving a life sentence in prison—not exactly the best environment to learn parenting skills. Hayward's conversion from criminal to caring dad was remarkable, especially when we consider how many people were so convinced that he would be the good father he turned out to be. Well, there's more to the story of Hayward's hope to be a good father that I think you will find interesting.

Malachi Dads

After Hayward's recommitment to God at Angola, his hope to somehow find his son and get involved in his life grew very strong. He had no idea how he would play a role in his son's life but hoped that God would provide a way. Hayward's desire was not just wishful thinking, although it may have sounded like it at first. He didn't expect a magical release from prison so he could be with his son—he hoped for an avenue to make that possible given the very real obstacles he faced being in Angola. He knew that would probably take a miracle, but he placed his faith in God's hands.

Then, without knowing anything about Hayward's hope to help his son, Warden Cain invited Awana, a church-based children's ministry active in churches all over the world, to come to Angola. It had never occurred to Awana, whose name is the acronym for "Approved Workmen Are Not Ashamed," that they might be needed in prison. They knew, of course, that inmates had children, but it wasn't even on their radar that this should be a part of their ministry outreach. In response to Warden Cain's invitation, the ministry's president came to Angola to talk about its local church-based work and was surprised when several inmates approached him for help. Hayward and other prisoners begged him to start a program there in Angola to teach them how to be better fathers. "We don't want our sons and daughters to end up here. Help us keep that from happening," they pleaded.

Awana is a suburban church program designed to teach mothers and fathers how to be better parents through Sunday school classes and midweek programs. They didn't have anyone equipped to handle a prison ministry, but Hayward and the other inmates were not deterred. They needed the tools to break the generational cycle of crime in their families, and their hope was that Awana could provide them with those tools.

The president turned to staff member Lyndon Azcuna because he had crosscultural experience and a commitment to helping fatherless children, deciding he was the closest thing to a qualified prison minister Awana had. Lyndon, having lost his own father when he was only five years old, had a passion for developing strong fathers and had worked with Awana for years to help children avoid the suffering he had gone through because of a lack of good parenting. Not having any idea what he was to do, Lyndon came to Angola and listened to Hayward and the other inmates who wanted to be better fathers. Together they developed materials designed to help prison inmates learn how to be there for their children spiritually even if they could not be there for them physically.

Then Awana raised the funds to sponsor an event, one day a year, when every child of every inmate who wanted to be a better father could spend the day playing at a carnival right there on the prison grounds designed to reunite fathers and their children. They had games, rides, and all sorts of other fun things that every kid longs to be able to do with their dad. Some of the dads had not seen their children for months; for others, it had been years, and for some, they were meeting their kids for the first time. The organizers decided to call the event Returning Hearts, based upon Malachi 4:8, which says, "and you shall turn the hearts of the fathers back to their children, and the hearts of the children back to their fathers." So then, it only made sense that from that moment on they should call themselves Malachi Dads.

In 2017, the Returning Hearts celebration at Angola had more than two thousand participants. Prisoners who had been permanently separated from their kids were able to laugh and run, to kiss and hug their children just like every child needs. On that one day, the inmate fathers of Angola are able to give their children the gift of their undivided attention and love. As powerful as the first event was (even the most hardened inmates ended up in tears), Lyndon knew these dads and these kids needed even more. So Lyndon began meeting with Hayward and a few other hand-picked inmate fathers, developing study materials to teach them how to be the kinds of fathers that their children needed them to be. Their goal was to break the legacy of crime that their children were destined to inherit and to provide them with a spiritual legacy instead.

Because Awana had never done anything like this before, and its staff members knew of no one else who was doing it, they had to do their own research and write their own materials to develop their program. Under Lyndon's leadership, Hayward and the other inmates wrote the materials and created the program now known as Malachi Dads, with their books and materials published by Awana ministries. Today, the Malachi Dads program is available in more than sixty prisons in the United States as well as prisons in Canada, the Philippines, Costa Rica, Kenya, the Dominican Republic, Cuba, and Haiti. The program has exploded because the need for inmate fathers to heal their relationships with their kids is so great.

Based upon the restorative hope of men such as Hayward, Malachi Dads has become such a powerful program to help detached fathers become better dads that freemen in churches began to hear about it and want to join. Lyndon began to hear things like, "You know, these Malachi Dads are better fathers than we are." So now, the Malachi Dads materials are available for use in churches everywhere, helping dads to restore the hearts of their children to themselves. As just one example, in 2017 a group of men from the

First Presbyterian Church of Baton Rouge drove an hour and half each way to Angola and back to participate in a small Malachi Dads group every single Monday night for twelve months. They graduated alongside of the inmates going through the program and joined the international community of Malachi Dads seeking to be the good fathers God has always intended them to be. In addition, Hayward and the other Malachi Dads hold events every year when men from all over the country come to the prison and stay there for the weekend to receive inspiration and instruction on how to be better dads. When Hayward began to hope he could be a better father, he had no idea what the future held. He just wanted to be there for his son, who needed him now.

After Hayward shared all this with me, I could hardly believe it. I told him that his ability to hope for something better in the midst of a bad situation was amazing. He replied, "It's about not settling for less. Not settling for what everybody else is doing. Not settling for 'This is the norm.' You know what? I'm in prison, but I'm not a prisoner. Because God didn't call me to be a prisoner. I made choices that got me here. But God didn't call me to be a prisoner. You know, I'm a man. I'm a man that can live with dignity, respect, integrity, courage—you know what I'm saying? And I can be a better person, right here where God has planted me. That's what happens when you get guys that buy into it. And that's what it is, a buy-in. We're doing what's right. We're holding men accountable. We are being held accountable. And we are changing lives. This community here, we stand together. That's powerful."

Now that's not wishful thinking—that's true hope.

7

The Difference between Religion and Spiritual Transformation

Since moral rehabilitation at Angola is based upon the Christian principles that Warden Cain brought to the prison, it is important for us to look at the role religion plays in changing the lives of the people there. First, we need to clarify a few things. What do we mean when we say someone is religious, and what is the difference between that and being spiritual?

The Differences between Spirituality and Religion

Everywhere you go on this planet, you will find people who believe in God. In fact, more than 85 percent of all humans practice one of the five major world religions: Christianity,

Islam, Judaism, Hinduism, and Buddhism, with Christianity being the largest. Psychologists have found that a belief in the sacred is one of the core human values that distinguish us from all other animals.[1] We are a religious species. It's simply how we are made.

Psychologists have also found that just knowing that someone is religious doesn't tell you very much, but you probably didn't need any psychological research to tell you that. You have to know *how* someone is religious to really know what that means. To clarify, spirituality is a belief in transcendence (which often includes God) that gives meaning to life and inspires personal transformation. Religion is the social institution of rituals through which spirituality is practiced. This means you can be spiritual without being religious, and, sadly, you can also be religious without be spiritual.

Sigmund Freud, the inventor of psychoanalysis, hated religion—even though he observed his own religious heritage throughout his life (even Freud had his own contradictions). He thought religion was something people made up to make their helplessness tolerable, so as a result, it made them inauthentic and defensive. Unfortunately, many psychologists and academic professors still agree with Freud today.

You might be surprised to learn that Jesus was very hard on religious people as well. He went so far as to say, "What sorrow awaits you teachers of religious law and you Pharisees. Hypocrites! For you cross land and sea to make one convert, and then you turn that person into twice the child of hell you yourselves are!" (Matthew 23:15). However, the difference between Freud and Jesus is that Freud lumped all religious people into the same category, and Jesus did not. Jesus and his followers believed that some religion is "pure and faultless" (James 1:27) and helps us to be more loving and better people. Freud believed that all forms of religion were excuses for defensive behavior to cover over irrational fears.

The truth is that the problem with the bad religion both Freud and Jesus criticized doesn't have as much to do with religion as it does with rigid thinking. Freud personally knew rigid, judgmental, self-righteous, and unloving religious people and assumed all religious people were just like them. Jesus knew religious people like that, too, but instead of despising them, it broke his heart to see them live such unspiritual religious lives. Psychologists have studied religion carefully and have separated out dogmatism (a way of thinking) from dogma (the content of what you believe). What this means is that you can be dogmatic about pretty much anything. People can be rigid fundamentalists about religion, politics, race, nationality, sexuality, and just about anything else you can think of. Once you become rigid in your thinking, you can use religion to justify your personal prejudices, but the practice of your religion will be anything but spiritual.

In order to understand this difference between spirituality and religion better, psychologists have developed methods of measuring the ways we approach religion. For instance, you can be intrinsically religious ("living" your religion as your main motivation in life, valuing a personal relationship with a loving God) or you can be extrinsically religious ("using" your religion, with utilitarian motives to gain security or social status). I have conducted my own research using this way of distinguishing between religious people and found intrinsically religious people to have psychologically healthy ways of managing their stress and anxiety in life.[2] Some religion is good; you just need to know what type of religion we are talking about.

As I mentioned earlier, it is ironic that the founder of the largest religion on the planet never intended to establish a religion. Instead, Jesus taught his disciples how to have genuine relationships with God and each other. He knew that some religion was good but also that religion is only as good as the relationships it exists to serve. In other words, the religion of Jesus was relationships—first with God and then with others. He was always saying things like "First go and be reconciled to your brother; then come and offer your gift" (Matthew 5:24). Practicing good religion was worthless to him if you didn't practice good relationships with God and others first.

Jailhouse Religion

We are all susceptible to jailhouse religion, not just people in prisons. Strictly speaking, the term is used to describe extrinsically religious people in prisons who are using religion to get benefits from the warden or prison system. Prisoners refer to jailhouse religion as the sudden and desperate piety of inmates who hope that God, or someone in the system, will bail them out. But you don't have to be in a prison to adopt this perspective on religion. I know of a number of people who beg God to give them what they want and are resentful to the point of not believing in God anymore when they don't get it. This utilitarian view of religion can put people in a spiritual prison of desperation anywhere, not just in our penitentiaries.

Since the Federal Bureau of Prisons reports that only a tiny fraction of less than one percent of all prisoners are atheists, criminologists are now studying religion in the prison system carefully. It is true that some inmates "leave their Bibles on their bunks" when they are released from prison and appear to have been extrinsically religious during their stay in prison. Some use religion as a shield of protection from violence, some use it to make themselves look good to parole boards, and others simply find the support of the spiritual community helpful in enduring their brutal circumstances. We will leave it up to God to assess the genuineness of their hearts, but we do know the practice of their religion drops off for some inmates once they leave the prison.

At the same time, I don't want to be too harsh on extrinsically religious people. I can think of a number of circumstances in which people turn to religion for comfort during times of stress but then fade away from God when their situation improves. To take an in-depth look at the various ways religion is practiced in our prisons, I turned to the work of Dr. Byron Johnson, a criminologist who has devoted his career to understanding the relationship between religion, crime, and incarceration.

More God, Less Crime

As long as there have been prisons, there have been prison ministries. Taking his words seriously, the followers of Jesus began bringing his teachings into prisons during his lifetime, and well-meaning believers have followed in these footsteps ever since. But it has only been in the past few decades that researchers have asked the question, "Is taking religion into prisons doing any lasting good?" This is the same question I wanted answered.

Johnson was among the first criminologists to look into this, and his findings were both disturbing and enlightening.[3] Yes, spiritual transformation in prison is life-changing. But what Johnson found in his initial research was that inmates who became Christians in prison and then were released into society were reincarcerated at exactly the same rate as those who did not become Christians in prison. This was very disappointing news to all the prison ministries when he told them.

But Johnson didn't stop there. He went on to further study the impact of spiritual transformation on prisoners and found that when inmates experience spiritual transformation in prison and then are integrated into a church or spiritual community after they leave prison, their reincarceration rate drops dramatically. As it turns out, spirituality is not a one-time event; it is a process of transformation that requires ongoing commitment. The Bible itself describes the process of salvation as both a single point in time as well as something that is ongoing into the future. It should not be surprising to any intrinsically religious person that genuine spiritual transformation involves daily encounters with God. When it comes to true spirituality, you are either growing or fading away. There is no standing still.

Johnson went on to do an extensive overview of all the research on the subject of religion and crime from 1944 to 2010. The results were impressive. In the more than three hundred studies done on this subject, 90 percent of them found a positive outcome between religion and reduced crime, 9 percent had mixed results or no effect, and only two studies (less than 1 percent) found religion to be associated with a harmful outcome. Interestingly, religion was often measured by frequency of church attendance. In other words, getting plugged into a community of people who are all committed to a personal relationship with a loving God, and making that community a regular part of your life, changes you for good.

What I am saying is that religious experiences are turning points, but spiritual transformation is an ongoing process. This is just as true in my life and yours as it is in the lives of the inmates who experience a spiritual conversion in prison. Why should it be any different? If you expect to keep growing spiritually and maturing in your ability to make good choices and avoid bad ones, then you need to keep nurturing your relationships with God and a spiritual community. It is just foolish to think otherwise.

The results of Johnson's work are clear. A critical reason that prisoners who experienced spiritual transformation while in prison and then ended up returning to prison for future crimes after they had been released was their failure to get involved in a spiritual community once they were out. It was that simple. Recidivists isolate. People who want profound changes in their lives to last don't. We should all take a moment here to consider this important truth. There are no isolated individuals when it comes to true spirituality, and certainly not ones who make consistently good choices. The principle is clear: if you try to go it alone in life, you are more likely to make bad decisions.

The research shows that church attenders in high-risk areas, such as crime-heavy neighborhoods, are much less likely to use drugs, engage in violent and nonviolent crimes, skip school, or get into trouble than their non-churchgoing neighbors. They are more likely to stay in school, make better grades, find steady employment, feel more hopeful, find more purpose in life, report higher self-esteem, and achieve higher educational goals. Johnson has concluded that these powerful benefits of living in religious community are not just the result of what religion discourages (such as drug use or delinquent behavior) but more the result of what it encourages—such as loving relationships, seeking a purpose in life, spiritual well-being, and valuing knowledge and education. Johnson has come to a clear conclusion based upon the overwhelming data from his years of research, which he made the title of his book: *More God, Less Crime.*

Angola Prison Seminary Results

Word of what Warden Cain was doing in Angola eventually reached Johnson and his team, so they sent a group of social scientists led by Dr. Michael Hallett to study the effects of the programs in Angola for a period of three years. They conducted thousands of surveys and more than one hundred in-depth life history interviews and published their findings in *The Angola Prison Seminary: Effects of Faith-Based Ministry on Identity Transformation, Desistance, and Rehabilitation.*[4]

In the place that was once the bloodiest prison in America, the very prison on which *Dead Man Walking* and *Monster's Ball* were based, Hallett found an inmate minister program that was among the most progressive in American corrections. Prisoners who graduated from the seminary located within the prison walls and participated in the fully inmate-run congregations (which existed at no other prison in America) had significantly less misconduct, reported transformed identities, and had a new commitment to positive social behaviors. These inmates were changed from selfish criminals to morally rehabilitated citizens of a world they were trying to make a better place, even if the world for them would be a maximum-security prison for the rest of their lives. And what was the primary explanation for this changed behavior? The number-one reason given was a spiritual conversion to a personal relationship with a loving God who they now knew cared.

Hallett observed the same thing I did when I was at Angola. The seminary was at the heart of this sea change in the culture of the prison. The more than two hundred inmates who have received degrees from the seminary are living and working among their fellow Angola inmates every day and changing lives. There are dozens of Christian denominations, and a few Muslim ones, holding weekly meetings for their members with vibrant worship services that I experienced as authentic and personally moving. And unlike anything I had ever seen before, Hallett also observed a striking culture of dialogue and diversity and a "measure of collaboration unparalleled in the free world."[5] These inmates had not been transformed out of fear of punishment by either God or the state of Louisiana; they had been changed by the experience of a spiritual encounter, and they were continuing to be changed by their ongoing service to others. They did not just stop making bad choices. They were now making "right choices for the right reasons."[6]

The Separation of Church and State

You may be wondering at this point about the legality of putting a Christian seminary in the middle of a state-funded prison, or the issue of the separation of church and state. The American Civil Liberties Union has been to Angola many times and even gone to court over a number of issues that they deemed important. But the seminary has never been one of them. Some may be upset that the only seminary at Angola is a Christian one, but they cannot deny the overwhelming evidence that the inmates there are changed for the better because of it.

Some organizations have been successful in seeing faith-based programs removed from other prisons, but that was because of the exclusive nature of those programs and the fact that special benefits afforded to the participants were not available to everyone.[7] But this is not the case at Angola. The seminary is run by Christian professors and paid for entirely by non-state funds, and it welcomes all inmates who wish to apply. Jews, Muslims, Catholics, and even an agnostic have all received degrees from the Angola seminary. Even the most hardened opponents of faith-based programs have had to admit that the Angola seminary is not an attempt by the state to establish a religion but is instead the recognition by the government that faith-based programs can be a cheaper and more effective way to accomplish its goals.

Warden Cain jokingly refers to the dominant religion at Angola as *Bapticostal*, in an effort to point out the inclusiveness there. Hallett concluded that the religion of Angola is best described as "relationship theology."[8] Even though the majority of the inmates do not attend any of the religious services, everyone at Angola is changed by those who do. The inmate ministers serve as buffers between all prisoners and security, they combat hopelessness, and they change the victim mentality that is so toxic to prison life. The level of freedom that these ministers have at Angola is unheard of in any other prison. This surprisingly progressive environment in the middle of America's regressive correctional system can only be explained by the fact that the relationship theology these inmate ministers practice is actually changing lives. Let me give you another example of what I mean by this.

Sydney's Story

"When I was first incarcerated, I was a very bitter man. I hated everybody. I was miserable. I didn't know I was miserable—I thought I was right, just like the world today thinks they are right. I looked around, and there was so much blood and foolishness on every hand. And I said, 'This is not what I had in mind.' How did I come to this point? I realized I was wrong for hating those people. It wasn't the judge, it wasn't the DA, it wasn't the jury. It wasn't my friends, it wasn't my family. It was me. And it was through this situation that God was speaking to me all the time; I just wasn't listening. I couldn't forgive anyone until I felt forgiven myself. God began to show me that if you desire to look into yourself, God will let you see. I discovered that I didn't want to be who I was. I desired to change. And I said to myself, 'If I never walk out of these gates, I'll never be that person again.'"[9]

Sydney was twenty-eight when he came to Angola. He didn't have a history of criminal behavior—quite the contrary, he was a successful businessman, but he let his drug-induced anger get the best of him one regrettable evening. That was thirty-eight years ago, and he has been in the Louisiana State maximum-security prison ever since.

Sydney grew up in a religious family. In his words, "I knew church. I knew altar call, and protocol, but I didn't know Jesus Christ." He got married early, had three kids, and was drafted into the military. When he got out, he decided to follow his passion for music, so he put together a group of musicians and built a ballroom. He was pretty successful, so he traveled with the band and developed a thriving business with his ballroom. But this late-night entertainer's lifestyle gave Sydney a taste for excitement that always left him wanting something more. The drinking, dancing, and other extracurricular activities eventually weren't enough for Sydney. So, on one fateful evening he made a deal for some cocaine. He wanted to take things to a new level, just because he could. As sometimes happens in drug deals, the dealer cheated him out of his money, and Sydney then made one of the worst decisions of his life—he went looking for him. He didn't find him, but he did find a woman the man knew, so he grabbed her and forced her to help him find the dealer. Sydney was angry, high, and seeking revenge. Looking back on it now, he knew he didn't want to kill the woman, but he desperately wanted to get back at the man who had cheated him. So in his anger, he raped her. Revenge is a costly emotion. The price for Syndey was a life sentence in prison, with thirty-eight years of his life spent in Angola to date.

Sydney had heard all the rumors about the violence at Angola before arriving there. He was ready to "take out" the first man he saw if the situation called for it. But what he thought was going to happen didn't. As it turned out, Sydney didn't have to fight for himself, but he did "take up" for other men at times. They didn't call it bullying back then, but the stronger prisoners preyed upon the weaker ones regularly. Sydney found this offensive and often defended the weaker inmates. Perhaps it was a way of expressing his anger, or maybe it came from somewhere else. But the only problems he ever had in those early years were getting into fights when he was "taking up" for somebody else.

Sydney was a loner. He didn't trust people. He was living the prison life, with drugs, sex, and everything else that went along with it, but no real relationships with anyone. Warden Cain had not arrived yet, so the spiritual culture in Angola was pretty shallow at the time. Inmates would cut out the centers of their Bibles to hide knives or pictures of naked women. A couple of inmates were serious about their faith, but not very many. In Sydney's words, "It was a lot of prison religion back then."

Eventually one of the inmates who attended a tiny prison church asked Sydney to join him, and Sydney just gave in, not really knowing why. Once he arrived, another inmate said, "Hey, we heard you could sing. Why don't you sing us a song?" Because of his love for music, Sydney gave in to that request as well, and the men quickly introduced him to their gospel singing group. As it turned out, that was exactly what he needed. Back in his musical element, Sydney started to feel like he was fitting in again. One thing led to another, and he eventually became a member of the struggling church.

A few years later, the pastor asked Sydney to lead a Bible class. He said he saw something in Sydney, and he wanted him to step up to the challenge. The problem was Sydney didn't know very much about the Bible. He had a copy of the Living Bible, and a King James Version, but that was it. That certainly didn't qualify him as a biblical scholar. But Sydney had grown to love singing in the group, so he accepted the challenge to lead the class, and he started studying the two Bibles he had. There were a few things Sydney remembered from having been in church when he was a kid. That, he thought, would be a good start.

Sydney had made what he called some "bad money" in prison, selling drugs and doing other things that he didn't really want to talk about with me. Because of the challenge to take on a role of leadership in his newfound church community, he was faced with a moral dilemma, and he wasn't sure how to deal with it. So Sydney took the ill-gotten money to the back of the building where they held their church services and set it on the floor. The only thing he could think to do was to pray: "Lord, you know I got this money doing bad things. If you forgive me for what I did, I will buy some books so I can start studying your word." The answer Sydney got was to go ahead and buy the books, so the first thing Sydney did was to buy a Matthew Henry commentary, then a Wuest word study guide, and then a couple of books on Romans. Once he started reading about the Bible, a passion sparked within him. Sydney found excitement again, only this time he didn't need any of the drinking, drugs, or the other extracurricular activities he used rely upon to feel good. Reading and studying the Bible became his new high. Sydney went on to buy twenty-seven sets of commentaries, including ones by Martin Luther, Charles Wesley, and Charles Spurgeon, to name a few. If he was going to teach the Bible, he wanted to know it.

Sydney started debating theological ideas with some of the older inmates in the Saturday-morning prayer meeting that was going on at the time. He was learning things and discovering verses that he hadn't even known were in the Bible. It was humbling at first, because he simply didn't know very much. But this just made Sydney study even more. Perhaps the thing that motivated him most now was the more he discovered about God, the more he seemed to understand about himself.

When Sydney became involved in the church at Angola back in the 1980s, the spiritual climate was nothing like it is today. At that time, the number of openly spiritual inmates was small, so they all met together every day of the week if they could. Sydney tried to be as real as he could with these inmates because it felt like they were all he had. They started having revivals on the yard and asking some of the gang members to let the younger inmates come to church.

Sydney had established some credibility with them because of those first few fights he had when he arrived at Angola. Ironically, it was Sydney's previous credibility as a man to be feared that gave him a pathway to establishing a new form of credibility with the inmates now.

Sydney is a good example of what Hallett found in his research at Angola to explain the decrease in violent behavior in the inmates there. Sydney perceives himself as someone with a new identity. He is not bitter anymore, and he's not angry at anyone for anything. In his thirty-eight years at Angola, he's only had a total of six write-ups for misbehavior. He's a model citizen, not for extrinsic reasons of hoping to be released for good behavior—as I mentioned before, that almost never happens at Angola. He lives this way because of how meaningful it is for him to have an intrinsically satisfying relationship with God. In his words, "When I started looking this way, I didn't turn back. I repented of the wrong I have done. I'm not bitter or angry anymore. I'm changed."

Today Sydney is the lead pastor of one of the oldest churches at Angola, and he is one of the coordinators and lead mentors of the reentry program that works with short-term inmates sent to Angola from other prisons to be prepared for life outside prison walls. Sydney's ministry is the life he lives alongside other inmates. When I asked him how he is effective with prisoners in that environment, he said. "Reliability. More than anything, trustability. When you factor all that in, we have believability. The current credibility that the church has in Angola has been gained because it has been honest."

But serious wounds leave scars, and Sydney is not without his. Because of his previous life, his wife divorced him, and his children cut themselves off from him. Of course, this has been a source of tremendous suffering for Sydney. His children refused to speak to him for years, and since his spiritual renewal in prison, Sydney has never been angry with them for it. Painfully, his youngest was only four years old when he was arrested, and he didn't see her again until she was twenty-three.

Warden Cain is creative with his programming at Angola, and one of his forward-thinking ideas was to establish what he calls a guest preacher program. Incredibly, inmate ministers can be invited to preach in local congregations outside the prison when their behavior has proven them to be trustworthy enough. It was on one of these preaching assignments that Sydney saw his daughter for the first time in nearly two decades. She told him that she hated him because he abandoned the family; he told her she was right to feel that way and admitted he had put his own selfish desires ahead of her and her future. He told her that he realized he had failed her and that he was truly sorry he couldn't change the past. But one thing he could do was to be the best father it was possible for him to be from that point onward, if she would give him the chance. Thankfully, she took him up on his offer. Because of Sydney's sincerity in that moment, and the irrepressible longing a daughter has for her father's love, Sydney has seen his daughter just about every two weeks since that day. His love of study inspired her to not only graduate from college but go on to earn a master's degree, then a PhD, with a passion for learning that equals her dad's. She is now a preacher herself and has been for the past eleven years. She trusts her father now, believes in him, and relies on him for the wise counsel she could only get from this man that she once hated and now deeply loves.

The way Sydney puts it, "You know you've got to practice

living right. You've got to really want to. I have failed my kids, failed myself, and failed my family, but I tell you what: I will never fail in life again. That is no longer an option. I am grateful for what God had done in my life and what he is doing even right now. I am truly grateful." Sydney doesn't see himself as a trapped person, even though he lives behind wire fences. You have to have the right mind-set to change, and now he does.

Sydney says, "We have to live for today. You can't wait until you get out to say, 'I'm going to live right, I'm going to change, and I'm going to go to church when I get out.' If you can't do that here, nine times out of ten you're not going to do it at all. Even after all ten of Job's kids were dead, he fell down on the ground and worshipped God. He didn't sit down and cry, he didn't ask the Lord, 'Why me?' When I read that I heard the spirit ask me, 'Can you worship in your pain? Or will you just sit here and cry?' So if I expect others like me to do it, I have to do it. I have to be able to worship in my pain. I have to be able to persevere."

Sydney has a surprisingly positive attitude for someone in such bleak surroundings. But when it comes down to it, life in Angola is pretty straightforward. It is impossible to pretend to be spiritual at church but then go home after church services and live an entirely different life. At Angola you have to walk your talk in order to be believed. Sydney is passionate about his relationship with God for the simple reason that it gives him meaning in his life. He is intrinsically religious because his personal relationship with a loving God makes it meaningful to live this way, and he gets up every morning to experience it.

"Yesterday's manna is not good enough for today," Sydney explains. "I need some fresh manna. I need to live for today. Every day, inmates have to deal with pain and losing their families. I just counseled two prisoners; one lost his mother, and one lost his father. I just sat with them this week, consoling them. Everybody here is your neighbor. We are just learning how to be one big happy family. I have one of the largest inmate congregations here. My co-pastor is white. When I came here, all the whites were locked up in one building. Then, Warden Cain arrived. He put his career on the line by opening everything up here. I don't tolerate racism. I already know I'm black; I don't need somebody to come and tell me I'm black. I don't deal with all that foolishness. I know who I am. Make no mistake about it—this is still a prison. And it's going to be a prison. But in the midst of this prison, there is a community. God is here."

I met recently with Mike Broyles, who works for the Awana ministry that has been so involved with the inmates at Angola. He was a pastor for forty years in a traditional church setting before he made the change to working with prison inmates. Now, working with men like Sydney is his full-time passion.

"I would never go back to working with people on the outside," Mike told me. "These guys are *all in*. This is where the true passion and commitment is in the church today. It is humbling to be around such depth of spirituality. I work with them because they inspire me. It's funny how it worked out that way."

From a psychological perspective, I think one of the reasons intrinsic religion changes people is because genuine spiritual transformation has the powerful effect of converting shame to guilt. We all live with some degree of shame, which is the feeling that there is something wrong with us and that we will be rejected for it if other people know who we really are. Shame is not prominent in everyone's life, but for some, like the people who end up at Angola, it is crushingly central to how they feel about themselves. If you believe you are bad, then you will act in bad ways.

The beauty of spiritual transformation is that it offers everyone the opportunity to be forgiven. But forgiveness is for guilt, which is the bad feeling you have for what you have *done*. Shame is the bad feeling you have for who you *are*. A spiritual encounter with a loving God who offers forgiveness frees you from your shame because experiencing forgiveness for everything bad you have ever *done* makes you feel loved for who you *are*. This type of genuine encounter with a loving God changes people on the deepest level, where their buried shame hides.

The inmates at Angola are dramatic examples of genuine spiritual transformation. Extrinsic religion just keeps us stuck in our shame; we act religious in hopes that our religious efforts will benefit us in some way, but our secret feelings of shame remain hidden and unchanged. Intrinsic religion is vulnerably exposing of our deepest feelings about ourselves and accepting the forgiveness of a loving God not only for our failures but for being the kind of person who fails. The fact that we fail does not disqualify us from love. This type of spiritual transformation heals us—not religious practices *for* God but transforming love *from* God. The grace of God heals shame, and everyone who is, in the inmates' terms, *born again* will tell you that.

8

Resentment Imprisons, and Forgiveness Sets You Free

Far too many people are trapped in the past by the incarcerating power of one of the most sinister emotions—resentment. Sadly, many think there is no point in talking about the past because no one can go back in time and do anything about it. But that attitude is usually what keeps them stuck. The truth is there actually *is* something you can do about the past. If you do it properly, you can forgive whoever hurt you there. Forgiveness is one of the only tools we have available to us for dealing with the past, but most people don't know how to take advantage of it. It's true you can't change the past, but you can change how you feel about it.

Resolving resentment is not easy. It involves getting underneath your anger, going over what happened to you in the past, unpacking your resentment, and forgiving those who have hurt you. Let's deal with the most common objection to forgiveness first. You may not even want to talk about forgiveness for the perpetrators who hurt you because they simply don't deserve it, and you might be right. But here is what you are missing when you think this way: when you choose to forgive someone, it is not for them—it's for you. Forgiveness is one of the most powerful and least understood tools for healing events that are sometimes many years old. No matter how difficult your past was, if you learn how to use this tool, you will have a better future.

Anger Is Energy to Solve a Problem

Because resentment is a form of anger, we need to start with a good understanding of that emotion. There are many forms of anger. Aggression is anger used to protect boundaries, and violence is aggression used to violate the boundaries of others. Hostility is an ongoing angry attitude that is negative and habitual. Hatred is hardened hostility that has gone on for too long. I think you can see from these examples of anger that failed attempts to express anger in healthy ways lead to problems. Every inmate in Angola can tell you that. But the most important thing you need to learn about anger is that, at its core, anger is simply energy to solve a problem.

Anger is a secondary emotion. This means there is always some other emotion underneath anger that is the primary feeling triggering it. The three most common primary emotions underlying anger are fear, hurt, and frustration. Of course, there are other emotions that can trigger anger, but if you can identify one of these three most common causes the next time you get mad, you will go a long way toward expressing your anger in healthy ways. Anger creates the energy you need to solve an underlying problem, and your primary emotions are pointing you to it.

It is important to remember that anger is an emotion, not a behavior. You can control your behavior, but you cannot necessarily control your emotions. If you are angry, there is probably a good reason for it. In most cases, anger itself is not the problem, but what you do with it can be. Anger is a powerful emotion that energizes us, but that also means it is potentially very dangerous as well.

The point is when you get angry—take care of business. Don't let a day go by without getting to the underlying reasons for your anger. Anger serves a purpose; you just need to figure out what the problem under your anger is and use the energy of your anger to solve it. Once we realize the underlying emotions causing our anger, then we have to undertake the emotional work of healing them. That's where forgiveness comes in.

Forgiveness Does Not Excuse Wrongdoing

Forgiveness can be mistaken for weakness or a form of denial used by those who refuse to stand up for themselves in the face of opposition. But this could not be further from the truth. Forgiveness actually requires a good deal of strength and a level of emotional honesty that is often difficult to achieve.

Let's start with what forgiveness is not. Forgiveness is not a fancy word used by those who are too passive to face the bad behavior of others.[1] On the contrary, forgiveness requires the acknowledgment of wrongdoing first. Forgiveness is for wrongdoing, so it starts with an honest acknowledgment of it. This is the opposite of denial of abuse or refusal to acknowledge hurtful behavior as wrong. Those who are simply in denial when it comes to dealing with hurt inadvertently wind up condoning it. This is clearly not forgiveness.

Good people do not condone wrongdoing; they get angry in the face of it. This anger is called righteous indignation, and it motivates us to take action against wrongdoing—because not doing so can sometimes do more harm to the victim than the abuse itself. Forgiveness is not condoning, excusing, tolerating, or minimizing wrongdoing. You forgive someone *for* wrongdoing. This requires you to acknowledge it, sometimes with righteous indignation, for exactly what it is.

Righteous Indignation versus Resentment

The God described in most religions speaks of a vengeance that is righteous and punishes wrongdoing with retribution. "It is mine to avenge," says the Lord (Deuteronomy 32:35), so the punishment of wrongdoing is a necessary and good thing if the world is to operate in an orderly and decent manner.

Righteous indignation is based upon the love of victims, and the love of good behavior, rather than the hatred of the wrongdoer. This form of anger defends those good people who have been hurt by wrongdoers who believe they have the right to mistreat others. In order for civilization to work properly, those who abuse goodness and other people must be confronted and put back in their appropriate position.

But resentment comes from a different place. People don't resent tornados; we resent other people who have done something wrong to us. More specifically, we resent being *demeaned* by someone else. Resentment is the anger we feel because of demeaning treatment, and resentment represents a personal defense of our self-worth.[2] Resentment is the hatred we feel for others who make us feel devalued, and it motivates us to retaliate in order to even the scales.

When an act of wrongdoing lowers your self-esteem, an emotional response follows. The two most common responses are the feeling that you deserved it, or conversely, the feeling of resentment against the person who degraded you. This resentment is defiance against the attack on your self-worth. But here is the problem: resentment is based upon doubt that has entered your own mind about your self-worth. Now you must protest the degrading treatment, and you cannot let it go uncontested. This attack upon your self-worth has shaken your confidence in your true value. Resentment motivates you to bring this other person down because that person is the one who deserves demeaning treatment, not you (or so you must insist). Resentment is the attempt to hide your own feelings of shame and cover over the injury to your self-esteem. Sometimes resentment even comes from your secret fear that you may have deserved this treatment, so you must protest loudly to keep your secret from being found out.

Righteous indignation is the anger used to stop the lies of wrongdoers claiming they are entitled to abuse others. Resentment is the anger used to hide the lies within your own heart that say you are now a person of lesser value. Righteous indignation does not necessarily make you feel better, because it isn't rooted in a personal feeling of insult that you are trying to soothe. However, resentment can make you feel temporarily better because its aim is to distract yourself (and everyone else) from your own feelings of diminished value.

Resentment is the outraged attempt to reestablish your self-worth in the face of an insult that calls it into question in your own mind. It results in a moral competition between you and the wrongdoer for personal value. You resent being insulted, and you feel entitled to insult the other to quiet your inner pain. This can make forgiveness almost impossible to achieve.

Righteous indignation is an issue you have with someone else. Resentment is an issue you have with yourself. The problem we have with forgiveness is not with our anger toward wrongdoing or even our desire for retribution because of it. The problem we have with forgiveness is rooted in painful feelings we have about ourselves that we are trying to cover over with resentment toward someone else. Distracting yourself from your pain by degrading someone else solves nothing. Recognizing the root of your resentment as stemming from painful feelings of self-doubt in your own mind is the beginning of a cure.

Once you realize that resentment is caused by your own doubt about your worth, you will be better able to take your focus off the people who have hurt you. Working on your self-worth deserves your energy, not getting even with others who have wronged you. This frees you to be able to forgive them. However, once you have resolved your issues with resentment, you still have to address the wrongdoing that has been done. But again, remember forgiveness is not condoning wrongdoing, because we forgive someone *for* wrongdoing.

Forgiveness for Wrongdoing

In order to truly forgive, we must expose the substitutes for forgiveness that we use in its place. Excusing is not forgiving. An excuse is something like "He didn't really mean it." Denying is not forgiving. Denying sounds like "It was nothing." Tolerating is not forgiving. We tolerate others by saying things like "Boys will be boys." Forgetting is not forgiving. Sometimes we will say, "I can't even remember what she said now." And even accepting is not forgiving. It is accepting to say, "That's just the way Mom is." Each of these might be necessary at times, but they are not forgiveness.

Because we so often mistake these substitutes for forgiveness, forgiveness can be mistaken for an act of either weakness or arrogance. Some people have criticized religious teachings about forgiveness as promoting the denial of resentment, which leads to unconscious acts of cruelty in the name of religion. And sometimes others are offended or angered by our pseudo-attempts to forgive them. The misguided attempt to offer forgiveness to others who do not believe they need it can be insulting to them, and they can even experience it as an act of superiority on your part. Forgiveness is not a tool to cover over your own pain or cause pain in someone else. It is based upon self-respect and respect of healthy relationships.

So, the prerequisite to forgiveness is the regaining of your confidence in your self-worth after some demeaning act of wrongdoing by someone else. This will help free you from trying to defend your value by pursuing some demeaning action against the wrongdoer. You may still have feelings of righteous indignation and even pursue retribution when it is called for, but you will need to dig deeply into your own heart to examine yourself for feelings of diminished self-worth that are the basis of resentment. Again, it is not the desire for retribution that prevents forgiveness but the presence of resentment.

The First Level of Forgiveness:
The Choice to Forgive

Without a proper understanding of resentment, you might think true forgiveness requires us to achieve some form of super-spirituality that calls us to live on a higher plane than normal people. You will be relieved to know that this is not the case. Forgiveness simply offers us an opportunity to free ourselves from resentment that destroys us from within and never leads to a satisfactory goal. Resentment is psychologically and spiritually dysfunctional. Any satisfaction we gain from it is temporary, and it only serves to lower our own self-esteem when we pursue it.

The first level of forgiveness is the decision not to return hurt for hurt. If someone offends you, you decide not to hurt them in return. They do not even need to know about it; this level of forgiveness is something you do within your own heart. You root out the origins of your resentment, deal with whatever self-doubt has been caused by the wrongdoing, and make the choice to forgive the other person. In doing this, you surrender any desire to compete with your offender in future acts of hurt or degradation because you are free from this pointless battle for moral worth. This decision affirms your belief in your own self-worth as well as your belief that other people have value. This means you can acknowledge that most people are not entirely bad, even if their actions sometimes are.

Resentment condemns the one doing the resenting. We want to believe it hurts our offender in some way, but most of the time it only hurts us. The resentment of others leads to the hatred of ourselves, while the love of ourselves leads to the forgiveness of others. Forgiveness is not some form of mystical piety; it is the decision to surrender your resentment of another person based upon your confidence in your own self-worth.

The Deeper Level of Forgiveness: Reconciliation

Let's say you have forgiven someone, but you later hear this person's name mentioned in conversation and wince with pain. This causes you to wonder, *Have I truly forgiven this person?* Perhaps you even spend more time trying to overcome the lingering feelings of resentment you still have for this person. Maybe you even need to do this several times. What is going on?

This persistent feeling of resentment that continues to haunt you points you to the fact that there are actually two levels of forgiveness. The first level is the decision to not return hurt for hurt. As I said, you can do this all by yourself without involving the other person at all. But there is a second level, which is the more complicated level of reconciliation.

This deeper level of forgiveness involves hard work with another person—something you cannot simply do on your own. Reconciliation requires a conversation between the parties that have been offended and an emotional engagement that seeks to resolve hurt feelings.

Because the process of reconciliation is difficult, all injured parties must have a mutual desire for a conversation to take place. First, you must get to the truth of the matter. Resentment must be replaced with honest emotions of hurt, fear, frustration, powerlessness, or whatever underlies your (secondary) angry feelings toward the other person. To do this, you must surrender the competition for value as a person with your offender and get to the vulnerable truth about how you feel. This requires great strength, because you already know you are dealing with a person who is capable of hurting you.

Then, there is repentance. This is frequently misunderstood to mean simply saying "I'm sorry." Often, when there is a serious need for reconciliation, the words "I'm sorry" are not enough. The ancient Greek word for repentance is *metanoia*, which means changing one's mind—to come to a new insight about the nature of your hurt and see it differently. Metanoia often looks like "I never knew you felt that way," or "I never meant to make you feel that way," or "I can see now why you felt that way." These are all expressions of a new understanding of the honest feelings causing the pain between you. Repentance wants the truth to be known, not painful retribution for past hurts or simple platitudes to cover them over.

Finally, the third step is a mutual understanding of pain. This is at the heart of reconciliation. Reconciliation offers us new insights and emotional understanding as we express our vulnerable feelings in relationship with each other. It is the experience of knowing the other's hurt and your role in it. This whole process is hard work, but it can result in the deepest level of forgiveness if everyone involved is willing to do it. If this whole process sounds too unrealistic or difficult to ever be achieved, let me give you an example of what it can look like.

The Forgiveness of Charles

Charles was born in Shreveport, Louisiana, and moved at a young age to Los Angeles with his mother where he grew up in the heart of the big city. As a student at Thomas Jefferson High School, he often sneaked off to do things his mother didn't know about. As a single parent, she did all she could to provide for and guide Charles without the help of a father (I think you can see this is a pattern for the inmates who end up in Angola). When he was around his mother, Charles tried to be respectful because she insisted on it. But he often turned to his peers for the support he needed when his mother was working long hours. Unfortunately, the group from which he sought acceptance was an inner-city gang known as the Crips. They were notorious for their violence and criminal activity, and especially well known for their ongoing war with a rival gang known as the Bloods. Everyone wants to belong to something, but unfortunately, Charles found his sense of belonging with the Crips.

After high school, Charles's mother decided to move back to Louisiana, so he offered to make the trip back with her for support, fully intending to return to California once she got settled. Even though he wanted to be supportive of his mother, his loyalty to the Crips had become a source of identity for him that he wasn't willing to give up. At first, he and his mother stayed with a few family members until she was able to get a job. But over time, Charles discovered a newfound popularity among his peers in Louisiana because of his association with the Crips back in California. There weren't any organized gangs like the Crips in Louisiana, and sadly, he was able to introduce this form of gang culture to his new friends because they all thought it was cool. Charles worked various jobs over the next few years and decided to stay in Louisiana to enjoy his popularity as the guy who imported the Crip culture to Louisiana.

When he was twenty-seven, Charles moved in with a woman whose daughter worked at a local restaurant. This daughter was having some problems with a man at work who was being inappropriate with her, so she called her husband to complain about it. The man at the restaurant overheard her call, so he in turn called his brother, expecting trouble. When situations like this arose, everyone knew there was one person you needed to call—Charles. And that is just what happened. Without hesitation, Charles grabbed his gun and jumped in a car to join his girlfriend's son-in-law, who immediately filled Charles in with the details. Within a few minutes, the woman came out to join Charles and her husband, followed by the man who had been harassing her, and the confrontation everyone expected got underway. Angry words were exchanged, followed by expletives and threats. Within a few minutes, shots were fired, with Charles fully intending to settle the matter once and for all.

At this point, the manager of the restaurant came out and tried to break everything up, claiming the police were on their way and ordering the group to leave immediately before anyone got hurt. In the chaos, Charles fired a few rounds in the direction of the man he had come to confront but accidentally shot the restaurant manager, fatally wounding him. This was an innocent man, just trying to keep the peace, and Charles took his life that day.

"That's something that I have to live with day in and day out," Charles told me. "There's no amount of peace I can really find for that."

Charles was arrested that same day. There was no doubt that he had committed the crime; everyone there saw him do it. Charles had been in trouble with the law before, but this time it was serious. He was going to court, where he would be tried for murder, and in Louisiana, that meant he would be sentenced to life in prison. Louisiana has the strictest sentencing laws in the country, and Charles knew it. All through the proceedings in court, he had a difficult time even acknowledging the people around him. He was focused on the seriousness of what was happening and how his life was about to take a drastic turn. It didn't take the jury long to come to their verdict. Charles was found guilty of second-degree murder and given the life sentence he knew was coming. Looking back on it now, Charles finds it interesting that throughout the trial, even though he was barely able to pay attention to the people involved, he couldn't help noticing the plaque over the courtroom that stated simply, "In God We Trust." Not knowing where else to place his focus, Charles found a sense of solace in that statement. *That's what I'll do*, Charles thought. *Trust God.*

Charles was sent to the Orleans Parish Prison in 1985 and transferred to Angola two years later. Remembering the plaque, he got involved with a few spiritual programs soon after he arrived and eventually started going to a prison church. There were only a few of them in Angola at the time, but Charles was sincere. He attended church faithfully because it was all he had left now. He trusted God because that trust was the only thing in his life that gave him anything close to a feeling of peace that he so desperately needed.

As I am sure you know, pursuing a spiritual path doesn't mean everything will go well for you in life. A few years later, Charles was told he needed to call home. He made the call and found out that his daughter had been killed at a school pep rally in a drive-by shooting. This was devastating news. He had trusted God, and this was what he got in return. He couldn't stop feeling bitter, and even angry, toward God. He wanted the system that had sent him to prison with a life sentence to do the same thing to the guy who had murdered his daughter. That was only fair. Charles lost many nights of sleep begging God for this retribution until he came to a sobering realization. Charles had previously asked God to forgive him for taking an innocent man's life, but he couldn't forgive the man who took his daughter's.

That sobering realization caused Charles to change his prayers; and he began asking God for help to get past his bitterness toward the man who killed his daughter. He prayed that God would forgive the young man because Charles had experienced God's forgiveness himself, and even though he never expected to ever see the man or know anything about him, he asked God to help the man find that same forgiveness himself someday. He felt good feeling like a forgiven man, and that good feeling of self-worth allowed him to surrender any need to get even with a man he would never know.

Then, a few years later, Charles received instructions from one of the wardens to report to her office. In prison culture, this is something like being called to the principal's office. Charles took a quick inventory of his recent behavior and asked himself whether he could think of anything he had done wrong. He didn't come up with anything, so he went directly over to Assistant Warden Fontenot's office to find out what this was all about.

"Charles," she said.

"Yes, ma'am?" Charles responded nervously.

"We have your victim's family here, and they want to meet with you. It's totally up to you," she said. "We are not going to force you to meet with them. That's a decision you are going to have to make."

Partly because of what he had gone through to forgive the man who took his daughter's life, and partly because he was trying to follow through with his vow to trust God, Charles responded with, "Yes, ma'am. I'll do it."

So Charles went back to his room and prepared himself for a meeting with a man named Bill, the brother of the man whose life he had taken years earlier. The guards took Charles to a little room up at the front of the prison. Sitting there apprehensively, he asked God to give him the strength to accept whatever this man had to say regarding the loss of his brother. Charles was expecting the worst.

Just as Charles finished his "Amen," the door opened, and Bill came in, accompanied by a woman and a guard. Out of respect, Charles stood up, and Bill said, "Charles."

Charles uttered out a nervous, "Yes, sir."

Then Bill said, "Charles, I have thought about you a lot in these past eighteen years. None of these thoughts have been good. But I have come here today to let you know that I forgive you for taking my brother's life."

Charles burst into tears. It was impossible for him to keep his composure, but he somehow was able to get out, "I prayed that God would forgive me. But I also prayed that one day the family of the man I killed would be able to forgive me for what I did. And now, here you stand. I can't believe it."

Instantly, that little cinder-block room filled up with emotion. Charles stood there with tears streaming down his face, Bill was tearing up, and Charles couldn't help noticing the woman behind him (who he would later learn was Bill's wife, Cindy) was tearing up as well. They talked for a while, and then Bill said, "You know, it has been good to see you, and I'll be back."

Charles felt like the weight of the world had been lifted off his shoulders. He went back to his room to thank God for what had just happened. Then it struck him: the date was February 21. He jumped up and said to the first person he saw, "Hey, do you know what today is?"

"Sure," the man said. "Today is February 21."

"I took a man's life on February 21 in 1985," Charles cried. "And here we are on February 21, 2003. The brother of the man I killed came up here today to let me know that he forgave me for taking his brother's life. God has done something here today."

For over fifteen years now, Bill and his wife have been traveling up to Angola a few times a year to visit with Charles. They both *want* to and *have* to. They want to because they have a new relationship with a man they now consider a brother. In fact, when Bill introduces Charles to other people, he says, "This is my brother Charles." He actually considers him to be a gift from God to replace the brother he lost years ago. But they also have to come, because Bill has reconciled his relationship to a man he had never known, but hated with every fiber of his being. The hatred Bill felt for the man who took his brother's life had consumed him for years, and he never wants to return to those days of bitterness and resentment. In a way, Bill goes to Angola not just to visit Charles, but to heal himself.

When Charles killed Bill's brother, John, in 1985, Bill was devastated. John and Bill were not just brothers; they were best friends. They did everything together. If John went fishing, Bill went along. If Bill went hunting, John was always there. Losing John was not just a sad event in Bill's life; it changed his very life itself. Bill was overwhelmed with anger toward Charles. He even tried to smuggle a gun into the courtroom to exact justice himself. He didn't care whether they took his life for killing Charles—getting revenge was all that mattered. Bill started drinking and isolated himself from others. He lost his job, and his hatred of Charles eventually cost him his first marriage. Even though Charles was sent to prison for life, Bill was consumed with resentment and a desire for revenge. *He can't get away with doing this*, Bill kept thinking. *He doesn't deserve to live.*

That's the way it is with resentment. What matters is not just what the other person did but how you feel about yourself. Bill's life felt worthless without John, and he didn't know how he was going to go on without him. He couldn't function, and he knew it was Charles's fault. Because he couldn't get his hands on Charles to make him pay, he was sentenced to a prison of his own for life—a prison of resentment he couldn't escape.

Miracles often happen when we least expect them, but need them most. When he was at his worst, Bill met a group from a local church that could see plainly he needed help. He was in pain, and despite his resistance, they didn't give up on Bill. They introduced him to the power of forgiveness that could set him free. It was in this way that Bill found healing for the years of hatred that had consumed him. Once he felt forgiven himself, he was open to forgiving others in a way that he never knew was possible. Bill now knew his life had worth because God and a small group of persistent people had loved him. He could see now that the belief that Charles had robbed him of a meaningful life was a lie. If you have a strong sense that you are worthy of love, no one else can make you feel worthless for very long. And since resentment is based upon the lie that someone has lessened your worth, Bill didn't need to resent Charles anymore.

Amazingly, Bill and Cindy did not set out to visit Charles on February 21, 2003. They were taking a tour of the prison in Angola that day, and they didn't even know that Charles was there. Bill had forgiven Charles and stopped thinking about him for quite some time. They took a chance and asked Warden Cain whether Charles was serving his sentence there and whether it was against the rules to talk to him if he was. Warden Cain looked into it, and the rest is history.

Every day, Charles wakes up with the awareness that he has taken away someone's husband, someone's father, someone's son, and now specifically, Bill's brother. Even though he feels forgiven, he can't escape the pain that comes with committing such a crime. There are consequences for wrongdoing, even after we have been forgiven. Charles wishes he could undo what he did, but he can't. What he can do is make good choices today and try to be the best version of himself he can possibly be.

Because of his good behavior, Charles was able to go before the parole board to be considered for a reduced sentence. When Bill found out about it, he insisted on being there. The board was delighted to hear that Bill was coming, as they always want to hear from victims' families.

"I'm not here to oppose Charles," Bill told them. "I have been meeting with Charles for several years now, and I have seen a change. He is not the same person he was when he came here. I would like to see him come home. He's done enough time." Influenced by Bill's testimony, the parole board cut Charles's sentence from life to forty years. In terms of parole-board hearings, this is a rare and remarkable thing.

Some people believe murderers don't deserve forgiveness. But what Bill learned is that forgiveness is not primarily for the other person, but for the one doing the forgiving. Bill lost a lot when John died, and he lost even more because of his resentment of Charles. But once he was able to forgive Charles, Bill's life got better. And once he was able to reconcile his hurt with Charles, his life got even better still. Forgiveness is a powerful tool in the hands of those who seek healing. It is one of the few things we can do about the past. We can't change what has already happened, but we can change how we feel about ourselves because of it. As I think you can see in the lives of both Bill and Charles, forgiveness is not necessarily an easy thing to do at times. But even in the most difficult situations, it is still the best way to be set free of resentment.

9

Does Change Really Last?

"Do you really believe these inmates would still live a morally rehabilitated life if they ever got out of prison?"

That's a question I am often asked when I tell people about my experiences at Angola. I don't blame them for asking it. The inmates themselves are very suspicious of jailhouse religion, and they are aware of the ex-cons who return to a life of crime when they get out. But is it the fate of everyone at Angola to only be believers behind bars?

The key to making lasting change is living in a new way—if you want change to last, you have to be a different person. This is not just following a new ideology or making a philosophical shift in your values or thinking. You must embrace a new identity and become a different person. The inmates I talked to at Angola had to change their identities from self-centered, hardened individuals to selfless, vulnerable members of a community. They had been living for themselves in the past; now they were living for God and the good of their community. They didn't have to *try* to do things differently because they just *were* different.

When criminologists studied the inmates who changed from violent offenders into peaceful members of the inmate population, they discovered that the inmates who experienced lasting change had a "re-conceptualized self-identity." Their personal transformation through great suffering had resulted in entirely new identities.[1] They didn't act in the same way they had before because they believed they simply weren't the same people anymore. They had changed, and as far as they knew, there was no going back.

So, the question we want to ask about the inmates at Angola is the same question we need to ask of ourselves: Does change really last? I think we have seen that change is possible. The lives of the inmates at Angola that I have shared with you are dramatic examples of it. After talking to each of these inmates personally, I came to believe that their transformations from selfish criminals into selfless members of a community was genuine. But even if change is genuine, can it last?

Forgiveness and Lasting Change

Forgiveness is a central feature of a genuinely changed life. As we discussed in chapter 8, the greatest benefits of forgiveness are not really for the other person but for the one doing the forgiving. Releasing yourself from a prison of resentment is a powerful benefit of forgiveness. The transforming power of release from toxic resentment would go a long way in solving much of the societal and interpersonal problems that we suffer from today.

But this is not to suggest that being forgiven for your own bad behavior is not also life-changing. I think we have also seen from the stories in the preceding chapters that once you experience forgiveness for what you previously thought was unforgivable, you are never the same.

When inmates arrive at Angola, they feel they have been given a raw deal. They feel like victims of a bad system—and, in truth, many of them are. I will never forget what one of the assistant wardens told me while I was at Angola: "The biggest difference I see between the prisoners here and you and me is that none of these people could afford a good lawyer." I was horrified by this comment, but I came to see that in many cases, he was right. This is not to say that these inmates had not committed crimes; all of those I talked to had. But so have many other men and women in our society, but they had the resources to hire the best attorneys who knew how to get them acquitted of their crimes. When you are poor and guilty, the system doesn't work in the same way.

Most inmates arrive in prison mad at the system and feeling entitled to a victim mentality. None of them claims to be morally innocent, but many insist they are not legally guilty (a term they have learned is legally defined as whatever the judge or jury decides). This creates a very confusing atmosphere of moral relativism and denial in which the true understanding of forgiveness for guilt gets lost. How can you forgive someone when they insist they are not guilty?

But this is where forgiveness from God comes in.

As I discussed in chapter 7, the problem the inmates have at Angola doesn't have as much to do with guilt as it does with shame. Whether or not they are guilty of their crimes is no longer the issue. None of them can change the past, and almost none of them can change the sentences they have received for their actions. But what every single inmate will have to deal with for the rest of their lives is the feeling of self-hatred. The feeling of shame, and the belief that you are worthless because of it, is a life sentence of hell on earth unless you know what to do about it.

Most of the terrible things people do in life result from feelings of worthlessness they have about themselves. Shame makes us act badly, and healing our shame is one of the most important things any of us can do to change our lives from bitter to better.[2]

Shame makes us feel worthless, but forgiveness from God gives us the experience we are worthy of love even when we don't deserve it. When this happens, we can acknowledge appropriate feelings of guilt for the things we have done to hurt others because we are no longer trying to hide from destructive feelings of shame that get in the way.

No one knows the power of forgiveness more than the inmates at Angola that I talked to. Once they discovered they were worthy of love and forgiveness, they no longer needed to act like people who didn't care about themselves or anyone else. They now feel they matter in the universe, which means everyone around them matters as well. When you feel like a new person inside, you don't act the same way you did before, because you simply aren't the same anymore. Not experiencing forgiveness keeps people stuck; receiving it sets them free.

Changed from Followers to Leaders

Many inmates at Angola committed the crimes that got them there because they were giving in to peer pressure. Some were barely old enough to be considered adults, and their brains were not developed enough to allow them to think for themselves. Like the young men in Zimbardo's prison experiment, the situation surrounding them greatly influenced the behavior they exhibited. We are all capable of evil actions, and when you are surrounded by desperate people doing reckless things, you are much more likely to engage in those same behaviors.

This gets us to one of the most important indicators of change in the inmates at Angola—whether or not they became leaders. Every transformed inmate I spoke to at Angola displayed the characteristic of quiet confidence, the kind that makes a person stand out from the crowd. These changed people were no longer insecure and looking for some nefarious activity to hide behind; they knew who they were, and they were not afraid to tell anyone who would listen. Each of them was willing to stand up to the most hardened criminals on the planet and lead them in a new direction if they would listen. They no longer followed the crowd or went along to get along. They had a new direction, and nothing, nor anyone, could distract them from their path.

The inmates I met who were truly changed people were mentors, teachers, pastors, group leaders, writers, talk-show hosts, and functioning in many other roles ready to assume responsibility for leadership. These people no longer considered themselves to be victims; they were survivors of tragic life events, and they had new identities that were strong and confident. I firmly believe if you put any of these changed inmates in Zimbardo's prison experiment today, they would fall into that small percentage of people who would simply say no to the situation, with a response of something like, "I'm sorry, but I can't go along with cruel behavior. It's just not who I am anymore."

Leaders don't give in to the situation; they change it. This is part of why the transformation in the lives of the inmates I met at Angola is lasting. They have as a part of their new identities a strong sense of personal responsibility to change a bad situation into a good one. These people are no longer looking around for someone else to do something when things got bad—they each feel it is their responsibility to be the one to stand up and take action to direct everyone toward good behavior. If you believe your life matters, then it becomes difficult to follow others down meaningless paths of destruction and self-defeating activity. Put simply, change lasts if you see yourself as a leader, not a follower.

Angola Is Changing

There have been some substantial changes at the Louisiana State Penitentiary in the past few years. The most dramatic one is that after twenty years as the warden, Burl Cain resigned in 2016. This decision was a complicated one for him, and we have discussed it several times since he announced it. Cain is proud of what he accomplished at Angola, in spite of all that he had to fight against to do it. Of course, he had to fight to change the attitudes of the inmates at Angola, and he didn't always win that battle. He is very honest in recognizing that some inmates refuse to change, and he will be the first to tell you that there will always be predators—prisoners who will hurt you if they have the chance. Not everyone responds to the opportunity for a new life, so fighting for the ones who can was never easy for Cain.

However, that was not the only uphill battle for Cain. He also had to change the attitudes of the wardens and staff at Angola. Prisons in the United States are primarily run with an atmosphere of fear and punishment, and Angola was no different when Cain arrived. Many who had been there for years thought Cain's policies of rewarding good behavior, providing formal education, and teaching responsibility to prisoners who had never learned it were liberal ideas for those who were too soft to succeed in the Louisiana Department of Corrections. And Cain didn't win all of these battles, either. He had a direction he wanted to take the prison, and he told me that the staff would either "get on the train or get out the gate" because he couldn't work with corrections officers who couldn't follow his authority. Fortunately for everyone, the culture of the wardens and staff at Angola did substantially change by the time Cain left, and he left a remarkably peaceful and violence-free general population behind.

But in the end, the biggest battle for Cain was political. He was so successful in his role as warden at Angola that, over the decades, he had become one of the most influential and best-known figures in the state of Louisiana. You can't go anywhere in the state without finding someone who knows who he is, and most admire his success. On one of my trips to the prison, Cain gave me a baseball cap with the words "Angola Chase Team" printed boldly on the front. He said I was to be an honorary member of the famed unit whose responsibility it was to chase down the rare inmate who attempted to flee the property. The eighteen-thousand-acre prison, surrounded on three sides by the alligator-infested Mississippi River, has been known throughout the South as practically inescapable, with most of those who have even tried to escape being caught before they ever reached the outer fence. Somewhat sheepishly, I wore the cap on my trip home and received a thumbs up, wave, or smile from almost everyone I passed that day. Cain is a hero in the eyes of the law-abiding citizens of Louisiana for transforming Angola from a place of terror to a place of positive change.

Cain achieved something amazing at Angola, but he wanted to have an even greater influence in changing lives. He was frustrated with how few pardons were ever granted by the governor, so he decided to take the changes he wanted to a new level and began thinking about how to expand his influence into the state capitol. So he formed a committee to explore the possibility of running for governor. For mostly political reasons, a local newspaper decided to take Cain on in an attempt to discredit him and prevent him from getting into office. They assigned an investigative journalist to dig up as much dirt as they could and eventually accused him of inappropriate business dealings with relatives of inmates at Angola. This particular journalist published several articles that made it look like he was personally profiting from his role as warden, which devastated Cain. After several months, and many hours of agonizing effort, Cain's name was cleared. In the end, each accusation was meticulously investigated by the state of Louisiana, and every single one was dismissed. Cain was exonerated entirely, but not before he felt he just couldn't take it anymore. He was deeply offended by the accusation that he was somehow acting inappropriately, and he especially didn't want anyone questioning his personal religious faith.

Cain is always thinking outside of the box, but he never acted unethically, and he didn't want to spend the remaining years of his life in the political arena constantly defending himself against these kinds of accusations. Cain was a hero to the changed inmates at Angola, and to the people in the state who believed in corrections being done correctly. But politics is a place for those with silver throats and the ability to say one thing believably while actually believing another. That is not Burl Cain.

So Cain left Angola to find a place of greater influence, but it wouldn't be in politics. He decided to form a non-profit organization dedicated to spreading his philosophy of corrections around the world. He has traveled to dozens of prisons around the United States and other countries preaching the gospel of corrections done correctly. And some are listening. Formed in 2016, Global Prison Seminaries Foundation has taken on the mission to spread the proven method of prison reform called the Prison Seminary Model. Cain, as the founder and CEO, began efforts to replicate his success at Angola in more than a dozen states in less than two years, and his goal is to have programs established in forty prisons by the year 2023.

Cain is convinced his model of formal education and moral reform changes lives. As a result of his efforts, other prisons are establishing their own formal seminaries, dedicated to producing what Cain calls field ministers, who will live out their sentences behind prison walls ministering to their fellow inmates through service and leadership. As he puts it, "The end goal of the Prison Seminary Model is to equip the long-term inmate, through robust and accountable Christian discipleship, to minister to fellow inmates behind bars for the remainder of their sentence."[3] Cain is passionate about his model for moral rehabilitation because he knows it results in countless benefits, such as fewer victims of violent crimes, safer neighborhoods, lower taxpayer costs, lower rates of recidivism, and most importantly—changed lives.

As you can imagine, some things at Angola have changed in the time since Warden Cain left. The new warden is supportive of the churches and seminary that Cain left behind, but the incredible freedom that inmates enjoyed under Cain was scaled back. That freedom is unheard of in any other prison in America, so it is not surprising that the new administration balked at continuing to offer it. Unfortunately, the new changes resulted in a decrease in morale and an increase in violence. To their credit, however, the administration recognized this trend and is working on reestablishing the programs and philosophy of corrections that were so effective under Warden Cain. The good news is that the inmates at Angola are still committed to their churches, their education, their roles as mentors and teachers, and, most importantly, their personal growth. Their reason for change was never because of their belief in Burl Cain, but because of the transformed lives they can live now. As Cain himself loves to say, "I'm not smart enough to do all this. I just opened up the gates and let God in."

The seminary is still operating in the middle of the prison at Angola, with new graduates entering into service in the prison population each year. The churches are still offering meaningful services, the mentoring program is still effective, and the special events such as the Returning Hearts celebration still draw crowds, with visitors coming from all over the state. And Angola is still sending out missionaries to other prisons, just as it has done in the past. For instance, the transformation of Hayward, who was instrumental in creating the Malachi Dads program, is so compelling that the new warden has sent him to teach men at another prison how to be better fathers to their children, even if they never expect to see them outside of prison walls again. Changed people change people, and Hayward is just one of many examples of this truth at Angola.

I believe the changed lives I witnessed at Angola have been changed for good, and they do not need Burl Cain to be their warden to make that change last. But what about the inmates who do get out of prison—will they remain changed once they are outside of the structure of prison life? Once they have all the same options and temptations that the rest of us have, will they stay on the committed path of moral rehabilitation that they lived on the inside? As you know, very few of the inmates at Angola get out alive. But a few are eventually released, so I decided to track down one of them and find out.

Eugene's Release

Eugene grew up in violent times, under violent circumstances. When he was barely twenty years old, in northern Louisiana, he beat a man to death with a pipe over a sum of money that he can't even remember today. Like it does for so many of the inmates at Angola, a single choice ended up costing Eugene the rest of his life. That night for him was March 11, 1956, an evening he will never forget, and always regret.

First serving time at the local parish prison, Eugene was eventually transferred to Angola in 1959. Despite his familiarity with violence, Eugene dreaded what was to be his new home. He was sentenced to life imprisonment for his crime, and everyone expected him to die at Angola. Almost all of the inmates there do.

"Angola will do three things to you," Eugene told me. "Number one, it will take you to a turning point. Number two, it will harden you. It will make you bitter and hateful, if you let it. And, number three, it will kill you. It almost always does."

Eugene explained to me that serving time in prison is like a two-thousand-piece puzzle, except when you are sentenced to Angola, the pieces of that puzzle are scattered all over the place. It's up to you to put them back together.

Over the course of his time at Angola, Eugene was beaten almost to death twice, witnessed murder several times, and lived in constant fear for years.

"Satan had the bill of sale on this penitentiary when I arrived," he said.

Angola was the bloodiest prison in America in 1960. Missionaries "would hardly even come in here," Eugene told me, because it was so notoriously dangerous. But one brave soul dared to talk to Eugene about God in 1963, and despite the hopelessness of his situation, Eugene found the forgiveness he needed but didn't even know he was looking for. He didn't know grace existed until that moment, nor had he ever felt loved, but grace and love changed him that day.

Pulling together a few friends, Eugene started the first prison church at Angola at a time when this was not the popular thing to do. Driven by his newfound faith, he studied the Bible and preached the good news that had changed his life to anyone who would listen. Eventually, "the spirit of death began to run away," he explained. With conviction and dedication that few people could sustain, Eugene counseled, discipled, and prayed for the inmates of Angola years before Warden Cain arrived to support him. His steadfastness was so well known in Angola that he became known as "Bishop" to everyone there, and the title has stuck to this day.

After Warden Cain arrived, things began to change for the better. Other prison churches popped up, the seminary started to offer degree programs, and the violence dropped off dramatically. Angola was a different place, and people on the outside began to hear about it. People of faith believe in miracles, and they believe that everyone can change if they are open to it. After serving fifty-one years of his life sentence, Eugene was blessed with a miracle that very few inmates at Angola ever experience: on August 10, 2007, Governor Kathleen Blanco pardoned Bishop Eugene and released him back into society as a free man.

Eugene describes being in prison as a "long night"—one that finally came to an end. I called Eugene several years after he had been released. I had to know: Did the change he experienced behind prison walls last once he was set free?

"People say that if you are in prison for over ten years, you cannot come out as normal," Eugene told me. "I agree with that. But for the person who has been truly born again, well, that person is beyond normal. That person has been extended to new heights by the power of God. People don't understand how I could be intellectually and emotionally normal after what I have experienced. Well, I am well and doing fine, and I'm more than ready for my new journey.

"God didn't give me liberty in my physical body. He gave me freedom to my spirit. A body in jail is better off than a soul in prison. I was never living in a penitentiary. I was always living in Christ."

The first thing Eugene did after his release was to move to New York and accept a position as a minister at the Brooklyn Tabernacle, because he had developed a relationship with the church's senior pastor, Jim Cymbala. The Tabernacle had been to Angola several times over the years, holding services for the inmates and supporting Eugene's work and that of the other inmate pastors. They were well aware of Eugene's ability to preach and minister to inmates within prison walls, and they were confident he could use those same gifts in the outside world as well.

"I saw myself walking the streets of New York many years before I was pardoned," Eugene told me. "I had never been there before, but I was given a vision. Even while I was serving a life sentence to never walk again in society, I saw myself walking the streets of New York. That is where I knew I was needed."

But Eugene didn't stop there. He signed up for training as a prison chaplain, feeling the call to reach out to others in prison, knowing full well what their needs were. And not only that—Eugene just knew there was a wife for him in New York. Now in his seventies, this man of hope could not be discouraged. After getting to know him, I was not surprised to find out that he did meet his wife shortly after he arrived in New York, and they were married in 2009. Both Eugene and his wife are licensed chaplains working at Rikers Island, a New York jail and prison of twenty-three thousand inmates.

Having served fifty-one years of his life behind prison walls, Bishop Eugene gets up every day and drives to Rikers Island and goes back behind prison walls to minister to the inmates there who are so much in need of grace and hope. Most normal people would be too traumatized to ever step foot inside a prison again. But Bishop Eugene is beyond normal. Just ask him, and he'll tell you.

He doesn't have the same access to the warden as he did back at Angola, and the tremendous mix of races and languages at Rikers makes his job difficult. Lethal race-based fighting happens at Rikers, and it is a challenge to get it under control. But nothing is slowing Bishop Eugene down, because he is a man on a mission with a vision to help these men and women behind prison walls.

At the end of my phone call with Eugene, he asked whether he could pray for me. I was so impressed with his authenticity and his prayer moved me so much that I felt the interview slipping away from me. I had called to talk about him, but now the conversation had shifted to being about me. This man was a pastor, and he couldn't help reaching out to care for me, a stranger living three thousand miles away that he was not likely ever to speak to again. We ended our conversation with Bishop Eugene praying for God's blessing on *my* life and with him expressing gratitude to God for bringing sunshine and love into both of our lives.

I actually choked up a bit as I hung up. Bishop Eugene was changed for good—there was no doubt about it in my mind. I believe genuine change can last because I have witnessed it in people like Bishop Eugene. Whatever the circumstances were that produced the criminal who took a man's life in 1956, the traumas and emotional scars that resulted from those circumstances have been healed. A selfish young man was changed into a loving mature one, and that change is a lasting one. Eugene is still growing and learning how to love. This is the type of person he has been changed into, and his humility and openness will keep this process of change going for a long time to come.

Some Closing Thoughts

Cain's Prison Seminary Model is not the only one in the world that is changing lives. Good things are happening with the Missouri Model, restorative justice approaches, and certain prisons in Europe that are experimenting with more humane approaches to corrections and showing positive results. This is good news for our planet. But this book isn't really about prison reform—it's about whether or not you and I can change and make it last.[4]

You have witnessed some dramatic examples here of how much people can change and how resilient that change can be. So now is the time to ask yourself, *Is change possible for me, and will it last?* What are the areas of your life where you need to change? You probably are not serving a life sentence for murder, rape, or armed robbery, so you have that going for you. But I'm sure you still have your areas of growth where improvement is still needed.

You are not a bad apple who is incapable of change. That's not you. But it takes discipline and perseverance to become a person of high moral character, and that effort never ends. You need to be a part of a community to make change last, so ask yourself whether you tend to isolate or participate in that area of your life. Sort out the difference between true hope and wishful thinking, and express your sense of justice with the desire to make things right in your life and the lives of those around you. Be a spiritual person, not just religious, and release the resentment that needs healing in your life. These are just a few things to consider if you are really interested in making changes in your life that last. The inmates of Angola have shared their lives with you in the hopes that it will inspire you to change your life for good. You have heard what they have had to say. You can change. The rest is up to you.

Endnotes

Chapter 1: Can a Person Really Change?

1. Alan Elsner, *Gates of Injustice: The Crisis in America's Prisons* (Upper Saddle River, NJ: Prentice Hall, 2006), 38.

2. Daniel Kahneman, *Thinking, Fast and Slow* (New York: Farrar, Straus & Giroux, 2011). Psychologist and Nobel laureate Daniel Kahneman uses regression to the mean to explain why we believe in punishment.

3. "America's Changing Religious Landscape," Pew Research Center, May 12, 2015, http://tinyurl.com /y2mojo4z.

4. Lisa Miller, *The Spiritual Child* (New York: St. Martin's Press, 2015).

5. Brené Brown, *Daring Greatly: How the Courage to Be Vulnerable Transforms the Way We Live, Love, Parent and Lead* (New York: Avery, 2015).

6. You might want to check out my book *Overcoming Shame: Let Go of Others' Expectations and Embrace God's Acceptance* (Eugene, OR: Harvest House, 2018).

7. Daniel Levinson, *Seasons of a Man's Life* (New York: Random House, 1978).

Chapter 2: Are Some People Just Bad Apples?

1. Philip Zimbardo, *The Lucifer Effect: Understanding How Good People Turn Evil* (New York: Random House, 2007), 168.

2. Zimbardo, *The Lucifer Effect*, 168.

3. I will mention this again in the next chapter, but there is a debate among criminologists about whether or not truly evil people have a neurological defect in the area of their brains that controls empathy. Some believe true psychopaths are incapable of empathy or guilt and that there is a neurological explanation for this.

4. Robert Hare, *Without Conscience: The Disturbing World of the Psychopaths among Us* (New York: Guilford, 1993).

5. Daniel Bergner, *God of the Rodeo: The Quest for Redemption in Louisiana's Angola Prison* (New York: Ballantine, 1998).

6. Jesus understood this human tendency to follow the crowd when he warned, "Woe to you when everyone speaks well of you, for that is how their ancestors treated the false prophets" (Luke 6:26). He was pointing out that the false prophets were often the most popular ones.

7. Daniel Goleman, *Leadership: The Power of Emotional Intelligence* (Northampton, MA: More Than Sound, 2011), Kindle loc. 188 of 1945.

8. Robert Greenleaf, *Servant Leadership: A Journey into the Nature of Legitimate Power and Greatness* (New York: Paulist, 1977). See also James Hunter, *The World's Most Powerful Leadership Principle: How to Become a Servant Leader* (New York: Crown Business, 2004).

9. Eleanor J. Gibson and Richard D. Walk, "The Visual Cliff," *Scientific American* 202, no. 4 (April 1960): 64–71.

10. James Sorce, Robert Emde, Joseph Campos, and Mary Klinnert, "Maternal Emotional Signaling: Its Effect on the

Visual Cliff Behavior of 1-Year-Olds," *Developmental Psychology* 21, no. 1 (1985): 195–200.

Chapter 3: How to Become a Person of Character

1. Andrew Newberg, Eugene D'Aquili, and Vince Rause, *Why God Won't Go Away* (New York: Ballantine, 2001), 109.

2. Robert Hare, *Hare Psychopathy Checklist—Revised (2nd Edition) (PCL-R)*, in *Encyclopedia of Psychology and Law*, ed. B. Cutler (Thousand Oaks, CA: Sage, 2008).

3. Hare, *Without Conscience*.

4. Daniel Goleman, *Emotional Intelligence: Why It Can Matter More than IQ* (New York: Bantam, 1995).

5. Robert Stolorow, *Trauma and Human Existence* (New York: Analytic, 2007).

Chapter 4: People Need Community to Change

1. Robert Stolorow and George Atwood, *Contexts of Being: The Intersubjective Foundations of Psychological Life* (Hillsdale, NJ: Analytic, 1992).

2. It is no accident that Jesus, the spiritual teacher with the greatest following on the planet, defined truth in relational terms. He didn't say, "I will tell you the truth." He said, "I *am* the truth" (John 14:6). He was urging his followers to seek a relationship with him rather than simply seeking information about him.

Chapter 5: Justice Means Making Things Right

1. Elsner, *Gates of Injustice*.

2. There are several uses of this term, but I like Derek Flood, *The Healing Gospel* (Eugene, OR: Cascade, 2012). Warden Cain is not a big fan of the restorative justice movement, per se, but he does practice his own brand of justice that focuses on making things right.

3. I want to clarify that Warden Cain does not identify with the restorative justice movement that emphasizes putting offenders and victims together for reconciliation. He is open to this, but he has his own approach to it.

Chapter 6: True Hope versus Wishful Thinking

1. Stephen Mitchell, *Hope and Dread in Psychoanalysis* (New York: Basic, 1993).

Chapter 7: The Difference between Religion and Spiritual Transformation

1. Jonathan Haidt, *The Righteous Mind: Why Good People Are Divided by Politics and Religion* (New York: Pantheon, 2012).

2. Mark Baker and Richard Gorsuch, "Trait Anxiety and Intrinsic-Extrinsic Religiousness," *Journal for the Scientific Study of Religion* 21, no. 2 (June 1982).

3. Byron R. Johnson, *More God, Less Crime: Why Faith Matters and How It Could Matter More* (West Conshohocken, PA: Templeton, 2011).

4. Michael Hallett, Joshua Hays, Byron R. Johnson, Sung Joon Jang, and Grant Duwe, *The Angola Prison Seminary:*

Effects of Faith-Based Ministry on Identity Transformation, Desistance, and Rehabilitation (New York: Routledge, 2017).

5. Hallett et al., *The Angola Prison Seminary*, Kindle edition, p. 183.

6. Hallett et al., *The Angola Prison Seminary*, Kindle edition, p. 205.

7. Winnifred Fallers Sullivan, *Prison Religion: Faith-Based Reform and the Constitution* (Princeton, NJ: Princeton University Press, 2009).

8. Hallett et al., *The Angola Prison Seminary*, Kindle edition, p. 220.

9. "The Miracle of Hope—The Brooklyn Tabernacle Singers," YouTube video, 09:08, uploaded by "Brian Zx," June 27, 2009, https://youtu.be/7A8C2V5xau0.

Chapter 8: Resentment Imprisons, and Forgiveness Sets You Free

1. Friedrich Nietzsche referred to Christianity as a "religion of pity" based upon his mistaken view of forgiveness and mercy as ineffectual passivity in *The Anti-Christ* (Tucson, AZ: Sharp, 1999), Section 7.

2. This chapter was greatly inspired by Jeffrie Murphy and Jean Hampton, *Forgiveness and Mercy* (New York: Cambridge University Press, 1988).

Chapter 9: Does Change Really Last?

1. Hallett et al., *The Angola Prison Seminary*, 234. Kindle edition, p. 48.

2. For more on this topic, see Baker, *Overcoming Shame*.

3. "The Prison Seminary Model," Global Prison Seminaries Foundation, http://tinyurl.com/y5sl2kra.

4. To read about important work on racial inequality and prison reform, see Bryan Stevenson, *Just Mercy: A Story of Justice and Redemption* (New York: Spiegel & Grau, 2015).